Henry Steele Commager

The Defeat of America

Presidential Power
and the National Character

SIMON AND SCHUSTER

NEW YORK

Library of Congress Cataloging in Publication Data

Commager, Henry Steele, 1902–
The defeat of America.

1. Executive power—United States—History.
2. United States—Foreign relations. I. Title.
JK511.C64   353.03'2   74–19472
ISBN 0–671–21776–3
ISBN 0–671–21777–1 (pbk.)

To
Milton Cantor
who has been the sounding board
for many of these ideas.

Contents

Introduction

These essays have a common theme. They are inspired by the palpable collapse of American foreign policy in the past quarter-century, a policy that carried us from the commanding position of the architect of victory, peace and reconstruction which we held unchallenged for some years after the Great War to the catastrophe of the Vietnam and Cambodian wars and the loss of world leadership and of self-respect. They seek to explain, or at least to illuminate, the implications of that collapse for our political and constitutional fabric and to interpret its consequences for our moral fabric.

The United States emerged from the greatest of wars bestriding the globe like a Colossus. Never before in modern history had a great nation displayed such a combination of energy and resourcefulness in warfare, magnanimity in victory and wisdom in planning for the aftermath of war and reconstruction. Then the clouds gathered swiftly over the horizon. The Soviet rejection of the Marshall Plan, the Berlin blockade, the Communist takeover in Czechoslovakia created—or dramatized the reality of—Two Worlds instead of the One World so hopefully, almost fatuously, imagined by Wendell Willkie. Within three years of the defeat of Germany the Cold War was in full freeze; it was destined to linger on and to dominate the foreign policy of great powers and of small for another two decades or more, and it is, in many of its manifestations and repercussions, still with us. The final defeat of Chiang Kai-shek in 1949 and the invasion of South Korea by the North the following year speedily gave to the Cold War a new and portentous dimension. With the death of Stalin came a brief truce in that war, but instead of trying to conclude a general armistice, the United States expanded the Cold War from Europe to Asia, from the Soviet Union to China, and then—under the aegis of Senator Joseph McCarthy—it was enlarged to embrace the American domestic scene.

Thus, by the early fifties, the Cold War had taken on a global character. For this development the United States was in part responsible. Confident that Providence had appointed us its chosen instrument to frustrate Communism wherever it threatened peace, stability and morality, we took our stance at Armageddon and battled for the Lord. Those who were not with us were against us, we said, and we used our prodigious resources of money and influence and, eventually, of military power to strike down the wicked and to inspire and arm the righteous, thus dividing the world into two hostile camps on the basis of morality.

All of this introduced a radically new principle into the conduct of American foreign policy. Not democracy or republicanism, not independence or the requirements of nation-making, not even sheer need came to be the criterion for winning American support, but open hostility to Communism. One of the more sobering by-products of this new policy was that it blinded us to the greatest revolution in modern history—the greatest surely since the Renaissance and the discovery of America: the revolution of two-thirds of the human race striving to emerge from five centuries of poverty and misery, misrule and exploitation, ignorance and superstition, and to catch up in one convulsive leap with the prosperous Western world. We, who were the firstborn of revolution, and who were in our youth the beacon light of hope for the peoples of the Old World and the fiery torch of danger to their governments, set our faces—and our energies—against revolution everywhere. We became what the Holy Alliance had been in the early years of the nineteenth century, what Britain was in the latter years of that century: a champion of the status quo, a bastion of power and of privilege, the foe of all who hoped to break away from the past and come out into the sunlight of the modern age. Under Eisenhower, and then his successors, we intervened to put down revolutions in Guatemala and Cuba and Santo Domingo and avowed our readiness to put it down everywhere; we rallied to the support of the Generals in Spain and in Brazil and of the Colonels in Greece and of colonialism in much of Africa and, most fatefully, in Vietnam. We were, to be sure, lavish with foreign aid, but that aid was increasingly military; what was not for the military was too little, or had too many strings attached to it, or was misdirected—as with so much of our aid to Latin America. Had we been prepared to spend money for peaceful purposes in Latin America, India, Vietnam on the scale of our expenditures for war in Southeast Asia or for atomic weaponry, the world, and our place in it, might not be the political shambles to which our policies have helped reduce it.

The decision, never formally debated by the Congress, to give the Cold War global dimensions and to make Asia, rather than Europe, its center of gravity had its roots deep in what Samuel Flagg Bemis at the turn of the century called "the great aberration"—the extension of the Spanish War to the Philippines and the subsequent conquest and annexation of those islands, participation in the expedition to put down the Boxer Rebellion, the Open Door doctrine—all bespeaking the conviction that we had somehow become an Asian power. We beat a partial retreat from this ground in the years from Wilson to Franklin Roosevelt, but with the Japanese attack on Pearl Harbor, the vast enterprise of the war on Japan with its ghastly climax at Hiroshima, the inevitable alliance with the Republic of China in the war against Japan and our just concern for Alaska and Hawaii, the concept of "Asian power" got a new lease on life. Once allied with Chiang Kai-shek, we felt ourselves irretrievably committed to him and his regime; once committed to these, we found ourselves inexorably caught up in a war not only against the Chinese Communists—who had an awkward habit of winning victories—but against Communism everywhere in Asia.

Behind this fateful return to an earlier and outworn policy lay a series of assumptions never seriously examined: that the United States had "vital interests" in mainland Asia and was therefore destined to be an "Asian power"; that Communism threatened these vital interests everywhere in Asia and in the Pacific; that Asian Communism did not differ essentially from Russian, that it was just as deeply immoral, just as dangerous, just as monolithic, and that it must therefore be "contained"; that Communist China was by its very nature imperialistic and militaristic, and that it directly threatened our interests in that quarter of the globe; that Chiang Kai-shek somehow represented the "real" China, and that—with our help, of course—he could return to the mainland and reestablish there a republican regime; that we could not only restore mainland China to Chiang but could somehow erect barriers to the expansion of Communism throughout Southeast Asia where—again—it somehow threatened our vital interests. Scholars like Owen Lattimore examined

these assumptions and found them wholly wanting in credibility or logic; but no matter. Our government in turn rejected the conclusions of the scholars and even punished
them for arriving at such conclusions.

To justify and vindicate this network of assumptions, the
United States built up its naval and air bases throughout
the Pacific—we had, after all, Japan, Okinawa, Taiwan and
the Philippines to work from; created a totally unrealistic
SEATO to give a spurious legal window-dressing to political
and military intervention in the affairs of Southeast Asia;
poured billions into the lost cause of Chiang; flirted with war
against China in the Pescadores; underwrote the disastrous
French war in Indochina and, when that collapsed, took over
from the French a war which proved in the end even more
disastrous and extended that war to Laos, Cambodia and even
Thailand. Much of this was done covertly; even what was
done overtly was never debated or specifically authorized
by the Congress. Rarely before in history had a great nation
drifted so mindlessly into catastrophe.

The rest of the story is so familiar and so painful that
many Americans prefer to ignore it or forget it or pretend
(as with the My Lai massacre, or the use of napalm, or the
hundred-year defoliation, or the Christmas bombings of '72)
that it somehow never really happened. We knew, but refused to acknowledge, that the war was fought for reasons
which no one in an official position was ever able to make
clear; that it was fought for no discernible objective except
perhaps that of avoiding the humiliation of defeat; that it
was fought with no support from our SEATO allies or from
other Asian nations, and with the use of large mercenary
armies—one of the things that both President Johnson and
President Nixon lied about; that it was fought with a ferocity
greater than we had displayed in any previous war, against a
people we did not know, who confronted us with no threat

and who had done us no harm; and that it was fought with almost equal ferocity against those we regarded as "enemies" and those we regarded as "allies." It turned out to be the longest war, the cruelest war, the most deeply immoral war and—with the exception of World War II—the costliest war in which we had ever been engaged. In the end it was clear that it had all been to no purpose, for we ourselves accepted the very Chinese Communism which it had been the ostensible objective of the war to contain. Mr. Nixon celebrated the formal end of our participation in the war as "peace with honor"; we can see now that the conclusion of the war was as dishonest as its initiation in the Tonkin Gulf episode, for there is no peace and there is no honor.

For all this Richard Nixon provides more than a convenient common denominator, a continuity, even a symbol. Probably no other American capitalized so long, so cynically or so successfully on the "Communist menace" as did Mr. Nixon, and none contributed more over the years to the national paranoia about Communism. Earlier than most Mr. Nixon had discovered pay dirt in the Communist issue. He defeated Jerry Voorhees for Congress in 1946 by the trickery of printing "pink" ballots designed to prove that his opponent was a Communist; he defeated Helen Gahagan Douglas by falsely associating her with Communism—and with Negroes too, for Mr. Nixon never thought it beneath him to cultivate racial prejudice. As a fledgling congressman he produced, with the now forgotten Representative Mundt, one of the first of the many anti-Communist bills, whose purpose was not to root out subversion (for there is no evidence that there was any to root out) but to dramatize the patriotism of its sponsors. He waged the 1952 campaign on the wild issue of "twenty years of treason"—a twenty years that embraced the whole of the New Deal and of the Great War, and a treason that was demonstrated by Communists like Franklin Roosevelt, Harry Truman, General Marshall and Dean Acheson; and he associated himself gladly with Senator Joseph McCarthy.

It was the Cold War, the transfer of that war from the foreign to the domestic arena and then the war in Laos, Vietnam and Cambodia that led inexorably to the follies, illegalities and immoralities of the Nixon administration. What was new in all this was not so much the trickery and duplicity (Mr. Nixon had not earned the cognomen "Tricky Dick" for nothing, and we should not be surprised that he managed so speedily to turn the White House into an Augean stable). What was new was the overt attack on the Constitution and the Bill of Rights, the unashamed subversion of those political processes which Americans had developed to enable the constitutional provisions to work. What was new was the usurpation of a war power constitutionally assigned to the Congress, and the full-throated attack upon the principle of the separation of powers; the contemptuous resort to secrecy to prevent either the Congress or the people from exercising their constitutional right and obligation to participate in the making of political decisions. What was new was the presumptuous claim that the President was above the law.

It is in all likelihood this feature of the constitutional crisis that future historians will regard as the most threatening and the most significant. For had Mr. Nixon succeeded in his pretensions and his ambitions, the character of the American Presidency would have been decisively and perhaps irrevocably altered, and with it the character of the American constitutional system. Such a shift in the center of political and constitutional gravity would have led logically to totalitarianism, for the power to commit a nation to war (something the other branches cannot do by themselves) is in its very nature arbitrary and autocratic. Mr. Nixon and his sycophantic camp followers have tried desperately to give the impression that Watergate, and all that it symbolized of the aggrandizement of presidential power, was really much ado about nothing: an unfortunate administrative blunder, an error of judgment, something regrettable but without any deep significance. This is, of course, merely another—and let us trust final—example of that duplicity which has characterized Mr. Nixon throughout his public career, and which seems to infect all those associated with him. Watergate—if we include in that symbolic term not only domestic crimes but crimes in the conduct of foreign relations—was the major crisis of the Constitution since Appomattox.

These are the interlocking themes of this collection of essays: the perversion of the American tradition of mission by the Cold War and the Vietnam War; the aberration of a foreign policy which ended up assuming that the United States should be, and in fact was, an Asian power; the quagmire of the Vietnam War; the desperate lengths to which Mr. Nixon and his palace guard were prepared to go to vindicate that war—and their own war power; the crowding crises which all this precipitated in the institutions of the Presidency, the Congress, the Courts and the Constitution, and in the political and moral system of the American nation; and the resolution of these crises by the weapon of impeachment which the Founding Fathers wrote into the Constitution, for it was the certainty of impeachment that induced Mr. Nixon to resign the Presidency.

The defeat of America which this book recounts was primarily moral. Such a defeat may have—indeed it has already had—a cathartic value. There are already encouraging signs of the rallying of the people against that "long train of abuses and usurpations" which threatened a new kind of tyranny such as Jefferson could not have imagined. We may emerge from defeat stronger in our understanding of the Constitution and in our devotion to it; more ardent in our response to our obligation to be vigilant against usurpations of power; more intelligent in setting the limits on power;

more magnanimous in the exercise of power and more mature in our grasp of what standards of morality become a great people.

Aspen, Colorado   HENRY STEELE COMMAGER
    August 15, 1974

Myths and Realities
in American Foreign Policy

Two pervasive and persistent assumptions have conditioned, if not dominated, much of American foreign policy from the beginning of national self-consciousness—a period which began even before 1787—conditioned especially the philosophy of American relations with and attitudes toward other peoples and countries. First is the assumption, or the myth, of American uniqueness—a myth which justified and encouraged the habit of isolation. Second is the assumption of the political, social and moral superiority of America—a myth which rationalized Manifest Destiny, mission, imperialism and, in our own time, the imposition on the rest of the world of something that can be called, without stretching analogies too far, a *Pax Americana*.

These two assumptions had a common origin and have had a parallel history. For almost two hundred years they have continually interacted on each other, and their consequences too have been intertwined. Once we recognize the

From *America Now*, edited by John G. Kirk, copyright © 1968, Metromedia, Inc.

similarity, even the identity, of these assumptions, we can more easily reconcile what appears on the surface to be a conflict between isolationism and interventionism or—to put it historically—between the stance that the United States adopted through most of the nineteenth century and that which it assumes today. Isolation and superiority are rooted in a common attitude toward the Old World and in a common body of philosophical convictions about the character of the New World and the destiny of the American nation.

What is the origin of these myths and what is their rationale? What shapes do they assume, what directions do they pursue, what attitudes do they encourage, what prejudices do they foster? How are we to explain their origins, their character and their vitality through the vicissitudes of our own history and the history of the modern world?

The notions of uniqueness and of isolation—two sides of the same coin—were born out of geography; not just the simple geography of the Atlantic and the Pacific acting as all but impassable barriers—that was obvious enough—but the larger geographical circumstances of the discovery of the New World. We quickly become hardened to words and deaf to their meanings, and it takes some stretch of the imagination for us now to remember that for almost three centuries the New World was indeed *new*—new, strange and inexplicable. It was new in nature, new in history, new in its people; and no military conquest, no royal decrees, no papal bulls, no literary gestures, no scientific theories ever could assimilate it to Europe.

Where, after all, had the New World been all this time? Why had God chosen to hide it from the eyes of Christian men; why had He peopled it with men who were scarcely human and who were certainly heathens? There were giants in the New World; there were pygmies; there were men with one leg, and men with their heads on their chests; there were men with one eye in the center of their foreheads, and men with scales or feathers, like beasts or birds; there were Amazons; there were hermaphrodites. Even more marvelous was the natural world—the world of gigantic serpents, of alligators, of sea monsters, of clouds of mosquitoes that darkened the skies—the world of tangled jungles and fetid swamps, of deserts that stretched into infinity, of mountains that towered fifty miles into the air and lakes as big as oceans.

Where had it been all this time, and why was it unveiled now, five thousand years after creation? Clearly it was reserved for some special destiny, though whether for weal or woe only the future would reveal. What was unmistakably clear was that the New World was not just an extension of the Old; as it was different in nature and in man, so it had a different history and a different destiny.

It was in the English colonies that the notion of uniqueness and special destiny caught hold and flourished, and this even though the differences in nature and in man that distinguished the two worlds were far less ostentatious in the English than in the Spanish colonies. But it was not nature that proved decisive; it was history. The Spaniards, the Portuguese and the French who came to the New World carried their state, their administrations, their armies, their church and their land systems along with them, and transplanted them as nearly intact as could be managed. Threatened as they were by the immensity and the hostility of nature in their regions of America, they clung all the more ardently to what connected them with Spain and France. But the English colonies represented a genuine transfer of population. The settlers along the shores of the Chesapeake or of Cape Cod were not the creatures of their home governments; they came pretty much on their own. Nor were they fearful of being overwhelmed by or absorbed by the native population. "We hope to plant a nation, where none before hath stood," wrote the author of *Newes from Virginia,* and that is what, eventually, they did. For it was not only the Indian of the New World who was different; in the end it was the European in the New World who was different, and that was far more important. As Stephen Vincent Benét's Dick Heron said:

> This is a world where a man starts clear
> Once he's paid the price of getting here.
> For though we be English, true and staunch,
> We'll judge no man by the size of his paunch. . . .
> For here is a knight, and a Newgate debtor,
> And which of the two will prove the better
> Can you read the riddle? I will not try.
> But we live under another sky,
> From the men who never have crossed the seas.
> I thought I came for a lump of gold,
> But I shall die like a squire of land
> With my sons about me, hardy and bold
> And something my own that I never planned.*

British America was, in a sense, independent long before the Declaration of Independence, and would have been independent without it. She was independent because she was different, and the difference had already put its stamp on her character and isolated her from her mother country— which was not really England but Europe.

It was, properly enough, not an English American but a son of Normandy, Jean de Crèvecoeur, known appropriately enough as "the American farmer," who saw this and explained it for posterity to read. He saw that the American was indeed a "new man"—the American from England and Scotland, from Holland and Baden and France, it made no

---

* From *Western Star,* by Stephen Vincent Benét (Holt, Rinehart and Winston, Inc.). Copyright 1943 by Rosemary Carr Benét. Reprinted by permission of Brandt & Brandt.

difference—for *ubi panis ibi patria*. He was a new man in that he did not pull his forelock to his betters. He was new in that he owned land and could pass it on to his children. He was new in that children were not a curse, as elsewhere in the world, but a blessing, for he knew that there would be meat and drink for them, clothing and shelter and material well-being. He was new in that he could worship as he pleased and govern himself.

The American was not, to be sure, wholly a new man, for being an American was a complex business long before Henry James observed that it was a complex fate. The American spoke the English language, observed (or refused to observe) English law, lived under English forms of government; and England was the mother country even for those not of English extraction. But all that made the struggle for independence even more compelling, and its achievement more complex and comprehensive. It meant that political independence would never be enough.

For political independence was not enough. The Great Declaration said as much when it invoked the necessity of assuming "among the powers of the Earth, the separate and equal Station to which the Laws of Nature and of Nature's God" entitled them. The crucial word for our purposes is "separate." Americans had to prove, and have always been busy proving, that they are indeed separate. With Americans of the Revolutionary generation independence was far more than political. It was religious, for it repudiated the religious establishment and substituted in its stead voluntary churches and the separation of church and state. It was economic, for it provided the largest and richest area on the globe for an experiment in agrarian democracy, and dedicated that vast area to free trade. It was social, for it did away with traditional class structures, abolished the familiar categories of aristocracy, bourgeoisie and peasantry (not, alas, of slavery) and inaugurated a far-reaching experiment in social equality. It was geopolitical—if that is the proper term—for it turned away from military solutions for colonialism, rejected entangling alliances and embraced geographical and political isolation. And it was moral, in that it repudiated the moral standards and malpractices of the Old World and set up a society which was to have new moral standards.

Nor was all this merely a matter of repudiation, for independence was not negative, but creative. It was creative politically. Americans were the first people in modern history to repudiate a "mother country" and "bring forth a new nation," and that gesture inaugurated the era of modern nationalism. Since the Americans established the precedent in 1776, some ninety colonial peoples have broken with their mother countries and set up on their own. It was creative politically too, in that Americans "realized the theories of the wisest writers" (the phrase is John Adams') by institutionalizing what had heretofore been merely philosophical precepts. They answered the question of how men make government with the Constitutional Convention. They answered the question of how power can be limited with a written Constitution, separation of powers, checks and balances and judicial review. They answered the question of the relation of mother country to colonies by abolishing colonies and substituting in their stead territories and states, all the way from Ohio to California. It was creative in religion and philosophy, in that it legalized religious equality and laid the foundations for universal education. It was creative socially, in that it ended formal class distinctions among whites. It was creative economically, in that it made possible widespread land ownership, raised standards of living and threw open jobs and professions to all men indiscriminately.

Certainly the deep sense of separation and uniqueness

which independence inculcated was positive rather than negative. No conviction was more widespread among the Founding Fathers than this: that the Old World was corrupt and decadent and that the New World must at all costs avoid contamination from the Old.

"Blest in their distance from that bloody scene," wrote Philip Freneau of the relations of Old World and New, "Why spread the sail to pass the Guelphs between?"

Why indeed? Why risk infection in these

Sweet sylvan scenes of innocence and ease . . .
Where Paradise shall flourish, by no second Adam lost
No dangerous tree or deathful fruit shall grow
No tempting serpent to allure the soul
From native innocence.

So, too, said Washington's favorite aide, David Humphreys, who likewise described the happiness of America in terms of isolation:

All former Empires rose, the work of guilt,
On conquest, blood or usurpation built.
But we, taught wisdom by their woes and crimes . . .
Fraught with their lore, and born to better times,
Our constitutions form'd on freedom's base.

Dr. Benjamin Rush, who had studied in Edinburgh and London and then settled happily in Philadelphia, where he practiced medicine, founded schools, guided the destinies of the Commonwealth, wrote essays on all subjects and became a Founding Father, never ceased to preach the danger of contamination from abroad. "America," he said, "should be greatly happy by erecting a barrier against the corruptions in morals, government and religion which now pervade all the nations of Europe."

No one was more insistent on the necessity of separation of the New World from the Old than Thomas Jefferson. A true cosmopolitan, he delighted in the music, art, architecture, literature and society of the Old World, and he was never happier than when visiting the bookshops along the quays or sipping chocolate in the salons of Paris. But Jefferson never for a moment thought that the pleasures and advantages which the Old World offered to its upper classes were worth the price exacted of its lower—worth the price in poverty, misery, ignorance, superstition, tyranny and war —and he knew that America had the best of it. To his old mentor George Wythe he wrote in 1786:

> If all the sovereigns of Europe were to set themselves to work to emancipate the minds of their subjects from their present ignorance and prejudices, and that as zealously as they now endeavor the contrary, a thousand years would not place them on that high ground on which our common people are now setting out. Ours could not have been so fairly put into the hands of their own common sense, had they not been separated from their parent stock, and been kept from contamination, either from them or the other people of the old world, by the intervention of so wide an ocean.

And seventeen years later Jefferson confided to his friend the Earl of Buchan, "I . . . bless the almighty being who, in gathering together the waters under the heavens in one place, divided the dry land of your hemisphere from the dry land of ours."

As Secretary of State, Jefferson had supported—though with some misgivings—Washington's Proclamation of Neutrality, the first of its kind in history. When he himself assumed the Presidency, his disillusionment with France was as deep as had been his earlier disillusionment with Britain, and it was his inaugural address that promised "honest friendship with all nations, entangling alliances with none."

His embargo was a daring but desperate device to avoid war with Old World nations, a device whose potentialities were probed but not exploited. The War of 1812 confirmed Jefferson in his passion for isolation, and in 1820 he assured his old friend William Short:

> The day is not distant when we may formally require a meridian of partition . . . which separates the two hemispheres . . . and when, during the rage of eternal wars of Europe, the lion and the lamb within our regions shall lie down together in peace. . . . The principles of society there and here are radically different, and I hope no American patriot will ever lose sight of the essential policy of interdicting in the seas and territories of both Americas the ferocious and sanguinary contests of Europe.

"Both Americas"! Here, quite clearly, is the principle which was to emerge three years later (and with Jefferson's formal blessing) as the Monroe Doctrine. What it meant then—and since—is that Europe and America were two different "systems"; that they had different interests, characters, civilizations and destinies; and that they should leave each other alone. This is the most deeply felt, if not the most faithfully observed, of American articles of faith. Implicit in it are both the great myths which have inspired American foreign attitudes and policies for a century and a half: the myth of uniqueness, which emerged as isolation; and the myth of superiority, which emerged as mission, and eventually as imperialism.

Even before the Monroe Doctrine, isolationism took on continental dimensions, and for no one more fully or uncompromisingly than the isolationist Jefferson. The Master of Monticello had from the beginning looked westward across the Alleghenies and all the way to the Pacific. He was the chief architect of those land policies which were to open up

the West to settlement by farmers, and he strove—in vain—
to banish slavery from all the territory west of the mountains. As early as 1793 he had planned to send out André
Michaux on a quite illegal exploration to the headwaters of
the Missouri; that expedition did not materialize, but ten
years later the expedition of Lewis and Clark did. Meantime Jefferson had doubled the territory of the United States
by the purchase of Louisiana and had ousted the Spaniards
from West Florida—a process which his successors were to
continue until all the Floridas were part of the United
States. James K. Polk, who accentuated isolationism and
added the first "corollary" to the Monroe Doctrine, was also
the President who presided over the "reannexation" of Texas
and the "reoccupation" of Oregon. Meantime the Russians
had been persuaded to give up whatever claims they might
have had south of Alaska, and there were threatening gestures toward the British in Canada.

Thus, within a quarter century, the Monroe Doctrine,
whose original purpose was to proclaim isolation, had come
to be identified with the principle of United States hegemony in the American continents. During the next eighty
years that principle was to take on both larger implications
and broader authority, assuming protean form in Pan-
Americanism; Cleveland, Roosevelt and Lodge "corollaries";
and Wilsonian intervention. In our own day the principle
has provided a rationale if not a justification for return to a
unilateral application of the principles of the Monroe Doctrine and for the most miscellaneous kinds of intervention in
the internal affairs of Latin American states. "Communism"
has now taken the place in the American imagination of the
"Holy Alliance." Just as President Monroe charged that "the
political system of the allied powers is essentially different
. . . from that of America" (and therefore irreconcilable with
it), so his modern successors, Eisenhower, Kennedy and
Johnson, have found "Communism" to be "essentially dif-

ferent" and therefore incompatible with the principles of the Great Doctrine. Just as earlier Presidents intervened in the affairs of Venezuela, Mexico, Nicaragua and the islands of the Caribbean, so their present-day successors intervene in Guatemala, Cuba, Santo Domingo and, through the Central Intelligence Agency, in many other South American nations.

The principle of isolation was by no means confined to the application of the Monroe Doctrine in these shifting shapes. It conditioned American policy toward the Old World during the entire century from the Treaty of Ghent to the First World War. At the outbreak of that war it counseled "neutrality"; and though the United States abandoned neutrality in 1917, once the war was won, neutrality and isolationism revived and flourished, dictating the rejection of the League of Nations and the precipitous withdrawal of the United States from the affairs of Europe and Asia. Disillusion with the First World War took overt form in the neutrality legislation of the thirties, and encouraged in many Americans a kind of xenophobia. Charles A. Beard was the intellectual spokesman for this policy. Like Jefferson, he was sophisticated and cosmopolitan; and, like Jefferson, his isolation was rooted not in ignorance nor in vainglory but in a conviction of the uniqueness of America and the corruption of Europe: if America allowed herself to be caught up in the ancient quarrels and wars which for centuries had made a shambles of the Old World, then she might lose her special character and her special virtue.

Isolationism, or the doctrine of American uniqueness, functioned not only in the political arena but in the social and cultural too. Perhaps most remarkable in the social arena was the attitude toward immigration and emigration. The United States was the first major nation to throw its doors open indiscriminately to all comers; the first to challenge the traditional notion of the immutability of national allegiance and encourage the transfer of allegiance; the first to place naturalization and citizenship within the reach of all new-comers. For over a century it lived up to the promise so eloquently proclaimed by Emma Lazarus' poem on the Statue of Liberty. Americans were able to welcome, alto-gether, some forty million immigrants, because they were confident that these could be assimilated, because they knew that what Crèvecoeur had said back in 1780 was true:

> In this great asylum the poor of Europe have met to-gether. . . . Urged by a variety of motives here they came. Everything has tended to regenerate them: new laws, a new mode of living, a new social system; here they are become men; in Europe they were as so many useless plants. . . . they withered and were mowed down by want, hunger and war. What then is the Amer-ican, this new man? *He* is an American who, leaving behind him all his ancient prejudices and manners, re-ceives new ones from the new mode of life he has em-braced, the new government he obeys, the new rank he holds. He becomes an American by being received in the broad lap of our great *Alma Mater*.

And Crèvecoeur added, prophetically:

> Here individuals of all nations are melted into a new race of men, whose labors and posterity will one day cause great changes in the world. Americans are the western pilgrims, who are carrying along with them that great mass of arts, sciences, vigor and industry which began long since in the east; they will finish the great circle.

In short, the millions who fled to the New World did so because they wished to separate themselves from the Old. They came here because they wished to be new men, and their identification with America was their regeneration.

Migration did not cease with the arrival of the Europeans on the western shores of the Atlantic. It continued all the way to the Pacific, for the West was to America what America was to Europe—with the fundamental difference that while emigration from Europe constituted a repudiation of the Old World, migration into successive wests constituted a vote of confidence in the New.

It was natural that, as Americans welcomed immigration, they looked askance at emigration. That some newcomers were disappointed in the United States and returned to their old homes, that others were ungrateful and went back with the money they had earned, to buy land or a shop in their native lands—these things were to be expected. But that native-born Americans should migrate to other countries seemed like a betrayal. This double standard for immigration and emigration applied with equal force to naturalization. Immigrants who did not at once give up their native citizenship and embrace American citizenship were denounced as "hyphenated" Americans—and to be hyphenated was to be disloyal. But it was taken for granted that Americans who settled abroad—in the "colonies" in London, Paris, Florence —proudly retained their American citizenship to the end of their days.

Culturally as well as socially the American asserted that he was a "new man." No sooner had the Declaration separated America from Britain than Americans threw themselves, almost convulsively, into the task of creating, or vindicating, an American culture. As Thomas Paine wrote, "A new era for politics is struck, a new method of thinking hath arisen." Now there were to be an *American* culture, an *American* language, *American* philosophy, *American* law, *American* arts and letters. "America is an independent empire," wrote young Noah Webster, "and *ought* to assume a national character," and he urged his fellow-countrymen to "unshackle your minds and act like independent beings."

Soon two pioneers of mathematics, Erastus Root and Nicholas Pike, were contriving an *American* mathematics; soon Jefferson had substituted the decimal system for pounds, shillings and pence; soon the Reverend Robert Davidson and the Reverend Jedidiah Morse were describing an *American* geography; soon one Amelia Simmons brought out an *American Cookery* "adapted to all grades of life." Meantime almost every man of letters turned resolutely to the creation of a literature which would be truly American. It took almost a century to achieve that, and it cannot be said that the other hopes or ambitions were ever truly fulfilled, but what was important was not the ultimate achievement but the philosophy and the passion that animated the attempt. America had to have a culture of her own because America was *different*.

It is abundantly clear that the myth of uniqueness carried with it, and all but required, the myth of superiority. For if the explanation of the uniqueness of America was to be found in geography and history, her character was to be explained, rather, in terms of philosophy and morals.

Doubtless the origins of the doctrine of American superiority can be traced to the Puritans, and to the commonwealth they established in Massachusetts Bay. That commonwealth was a New Jerusalem, it was Zion, it was a City set upon a Hill, and its people were the Chosen People, for "God sifted a whole nation, that he might send choice grain over into the Wilderness." It is a sentiment that echoed down the corridors of history. "What great things has the God of Providence done for our race," said the Reverend John Rodgers in 1784. "By the revolution we this day celebrate he has provided an asylum for the oppressed . . . and in due time the universal establishment of the Messiah's kingdom." And there is more than a hint of the sifted-grain theory in the motto of the California Society: "The cowards never started, and the weak died on the way." Nor was it the Puritans alone who could claim to be a community of saints, but all who sought out a wilderness for righteousness' sake from Plymouth and Massachusetts Bay and the Providence Plantations to New Harmony and the Amana Colony and the new commonwealth of the Latter Day Saints in distant Deseret. But it was not merely the religious or the utopian communities that were Holy Communities. Was not all of America a Holy Commonwealth? So Americans could believe, and so many did.

As, over the years, the religious justification for separatism and saintliness evaporated, it was replaced by secular arguments grounded on fact and experience rather than on faith. *Amerika du hast es besser,* wrote the aged Goethe, and that was a visible fact that almost every white American could accept as the common sense of the matter. For it was obvious that America was better than Europe, her soil more fertile, her climate more favorable, her resources inexhaustible, her expanse limitless. Clearly, too, the government and society of the New World were more enlightened, more benevolent and more humane than anything the Old World had to offer—at least for those lucky enough to be white. Every schoolboy could recite the catalog of American virtue and good fortune: no kings, no aristocracy, no established church, no Inquisition, no faggot, no rack, no standing armies, no wars, no useless riches, no hopeless poverty, no dark ignorance, no flaunting vice. And these were merely the negative manifestations of good fortune—and good sense. Put it all positively, and the argument is even more impressive: instead of tyranny, self-government; instead of the Inquisition, religious freedom; instead of poverty, a general well-being; instead of classes, equality; instead of ignorance, universal education; instead of vast armies living on war, universal peace; instead of great cities with fetid slums, a boundless expanse of virgin land; instead of vice rioting in every street and flaunting itself in every salon, virtue and innocence. These were all articles of faith. There were other tests, no less persuasive. There was the test of progress—that was one everybody could understand. Americans gave to progress a new definition and a new meaning: improvement in the material welfare of the average man. There was the visible fact of population growth. Where, in the Old World, population barely held its own, in the New World it doubled every twenty-five years. That was true of the eighteenth century; if the nineteenth closed the gap between Old World and New in this matter of natural increase, it gave America a new advantage through large-scale immigration; and all through that century the young United States overtook Old World nations, one after another. Or there was the phenomenon of expansion more rapid than that of any other nation, expansion not merely through territorial conquest but by occupation. No wonder Americans came to assume that it was their Manifest Destiny to occupy the whole of North America. There was even the test of economic wealth and industrial might that the ebullient Andrew Carnegie celebrated in his well-named *Triumphant Democracy:* "The old nations of the earth creep on at a snail's pace; the Republic thunders past with the rush of the express."

There was exaggeration in all this, to be sure, exaggeration and a willful ignoring of slavery and racial prejudices, and much else besides. And there was self-deception as well. But there was still enough reality to give some substance to a myth of superiority which flourished for almost two centuries. What insured vitality to this myth was that by a natural, almost an inevitable, association, the superiority of the New World rubbed off on those who were fortunate enough to be part of it—not only the "huddled masses yearning to breathe free" who had deliberately chosen America but the native-born as well. They took credit not only for the superiority of government and institutions but for the superiority of nature, and complacently regarded the peace, prosperity and progress of the New World as somehow a tribute to their own wisdom and virtue.

The principle of the moral superiority of the American people found most eloquent expression in the doctrines of mission and Manifest Destiny. The notion of mission began, naturally enough, at the time of independence, and hints of it can be found in the most famous of all documents. It is "all men" who are created equal—not just Englishmen—and who are endowed by their Creator with "unalienable Rights." The Great Declaration appealed irresistibly to European *philosophes,* as did the constitutions and bills of rights of such states as Virginia and Massachusetts. Soon Turgot was writing:

> This people is the hope of the human race. It may become the model. It ought to show the world by facts that man can be free and yet peaceful, and may dispense with the chains in which tyrants and knaves of every color have presumed to bind them. The American should be an example of political, religious, commercial, and industrial liberty.

The Americans rejoiced in the role which history had thus assigned them, and prepared to play it. They held out—somewhat tentatively, to be sure—the hand of friendship to the revolutionary leaders of France. They encouraged, though they did not aid, revolution in Latin America, and were the first to recognize the independence of Spain's former colonies. Latin American revolutions owed less to the American than to the French Revolution, and Latin American independence less to the Monroe Doctrine than to the policies of George Canning; but Americans liked to think that theirs was the flame and the inspiration.

The American mission was to spread the principles of democracy and of freedom throughout the globe; the method was not force but example; and leaders of revolutions in South America, Greece, Hungary and Ireland who counted on more than sympathy were speedily put right. Not indeed until 1898 did the United States intervene actively in support of a revolution against a European "tyrant," and then (as in 1941) it was fortuity rather than principle that cast the decisive vote.

Manifest Destiny was another matter—the manifest destiny of the American nation to spread westward to the Pacific and—if the cost was not excessive—northward and southward as well. The story is familiar enough and need not be retold: the purchase of Louisiana; ousting the Spaniards from the Floridas; the annexation of Texas, followed by war over a boundary dispute which ended with the annexation of over half a million square miles of Mexican Territory; maneuvering the Russians out of the Pacific Northwest, and then the British and then the purchase of Alaska; establishment of hegemony in the Caribbean and the acquisition ("annexation" is too rude a term) of the Panama Canal territory. Here is a story of expansion, conquest and aggrandizement without parallel in modern history; yet to this day most Americans are convinced that American expansion was peaceful, and that only Old World nations— and now China, of course—were guilty of aggrandizement, conquest and imperialism.

Manifest Destiny and mission converged in what has been called the Great Aberration but what was really a logical product of both: the Spanish and the Philippine wars. Ever since Jefferson's day the United States had cast covetous eyes on Cuba, and fear that Britain might extend her sphere of influence over that island played some part in the formulation of the Monroe Doctrine. Thirty years later the Ostend Manifesto asserted boldly that "from the peculiarity of its geographical position . . . Cuba is as necessary to the North American republic as any of its present members, and belongs naturally to that great family of States." The Grant administration witnessed abortive attempts to annex both Cuba and Santo Domingo. In the nineties the spectacle of Cubans struggling heroically against their Spanish rulers touched the sympathies of Americans and added humanitarian to political and strategic considerations to dictate intervention. In a lightning war they ousted the Spaniards from Cuba and assured that island independence —of a sort; in the process they picked up Puerto Rico in the Caribbean, and the Philippine Islands off the coast of China, while a willing Hawaii fell into their convenient lap. Annexation of the Philippines was not permanent, but historically it was the most significant product of the Spanish War.

Myth and realism had united to bring about annexation of the islands. No one (unless Theodore Roosevelt or Admiral Mahan) had thought that the Philippine Islands were a logical part of an American empire, chiefly because no one had thought much about an American empire. But when, on that May morning of 1898, the islands fell to Admiral Dewey, and when the Filipinos under the patriotic Aguinaldo joined with the Americans to overthrow Spanish misrule and win their own independence, President McKinley and the American people were confronted with a wholly new problem. It is probable that President McKinley decided on annexation before he hit on its logic or justification; but when he did formulate this, it so happily combined mission and Manifest Destiny as to satisfy all but the most intransigent. "We could not turn the islands over to France or Germany, our commercial rivals—that would be bad business and discreditable. We could not give them back to Spain—that would be cowardly and dishonorable. We could not leave them to themselves—they were unfit for self-government. . . . There was nothing left for us to do but to take them all, and to educate the Filipinos, uplift them and Christianize them." Business, strategy and mission, with education and religion thrown in as a bonus—here they are, all jumbled together; and they have been jumbled together ever since.

There was an added complication when it was discovered that the Filipinos did not really want to be an item in American Manifest Destiny and fought for three years for their independence. "Beneath the starry flag, civilize them with a Krag," American soldiers sang as they proceeded with their new Krag rifles to give the Filipinos a foretaste of what the Vietnamese would get sixty years later when they too proved impervious to the claims of American benevolence.

The curious interplay of uniqueness and superiority emerged a decade or so later with the outbreak of the Great War in Europe. President Wilson met the challenge of that war with a proclamation calling upon the American people to support isolation. He permitted his party to campaign for his re-election on the program that "he kept us out of war"; he called for "peace without victory"; and he announced, on the eve of our entrance into the war, that there was such a thing as being too proud to fight. From 1914 to 1917 isolation was cherished and observed, because it was based, ultimately, on moral considerations. But when the nature of the war changed, a new set of considerations came into play— considerations not alone of strategic security but of moral security. Now moral arguments rationalized what strategic arguments necessitated and gave to the enterprise of war an exalted moral character. "It is a fearful thing," said President Wilson, "to lead this peaceful people into war. . . . But the right is more precious than peace, and we shall fight . . . to make the world itself at last free." It was Germany's unrestricted U-boat warfare that was the legal *casus belli;* but the war was not fought merely to restore international law. Rather, it was fought "to secure the rights of nations, great and small, and the privilege of men everywhere to choose their way of life and of obedience," for "the world must be made safe for democracy."

Thus, to preserve isolation, Wilson led his nation into a crusade which took on global dimensions. The crusade was successful enough in the defeat of the Central Powers; but it was not successful in its moral aims, and its failure to achieve these led, ineluctably, to the revival of isolationism. That the isolationism of the twenties and the thirties had strong moral overtones is notorious. Animated by the noblest of motives, fired by the most ardent zeal, Americans had launched a crusade to make the world safe for democracy. They had won the war; but, confronted by the wily diplomats of the Old World, by secret treaties, by selfishness, ambition and greed, they lost the peace. How familiar it all was: American innocence confronted by European depravity! In righteous indignation Americans rejected the treaty which their President had negotiated, because it was a treaty flawed by greed and vindictiveness. They rejected the League of Nations too, because it threatened both their isolation and their Monroe Doctrine and because it threatened to involve them, willy-nilly, in the future quarrels of the wicked Old World. So once again Americans retired into isolation. They had been for a time too proud to fight; now they were too proud to be associated with nations whose standards of honor were less exalted than their own.

Isolation and the consciousness of moral superiority persisted all through the thirties, even in the face of totalitarian aggression in Europe and Asia; and they account for the tardiness of American participation. The overwhelming majority of Americans were deeply shocked by the wickedness of the Nazi and Fascist regimes, but the majority of them denied responsibility and feared involvement. "We told you so," they seemed to say to the quondam internationalists. "This is what you must expect from the corrupt and decadent people of the Old World. Let us have no part of it. Let us be an island of civilization in an ocean of anarchy, so that when the holocaust is over, there will survive on this continent one nation that has not been physically or morally exhausted, and that will be able to restore civilization in a stricken globe." And notwithstanding that President Roosevelt moved steadily toward a working, and even fighting, arrangement with the Allied Powers, neutrality remained the official and the popular American position until Pearl Harbor settled the issue once and for all.

These myths of innocence and of superiority were, almost from the beginning, battered by reality. For the United States was never really isolated—not geographically, politically, socially or economically, and certainly not culturally. No sooner had the Treaty of Paris been signed, in 1783, than the new United States had to vindicate her territorial integrity from Spain and from Britain. She was caught up in the French Revolution, and when political parties emerged, it was to take sides on that conflict. She was threatened by Napoleon in the Carribbean and in Louisiana. She was assailed on the high seas by both the great contending powers, and in 1812 she had to fight once again to vindicate independence. The War of 1812 cleared the air politically, and thereafter for almost a century the United States enjoyed immunity from more overt involvement in European wars. But there was still the problem of clearing the continent of foreign rivals—the Spaniards, the British and the Russians — and not until 1867 could it be said that the United States had all the territory she had any right to expect! Economic involvement too was continuous, for the United States depended on Europe for markets and for credit. Socially the connection was massive, for every immigrant brought with him part of his own culture—his language, his religion, the habits he had acquired, the skills he had learned and the resentments he nursed. This applied with special force to Negroes from Africa or the West Indies; and their descendants have to this day retained some of their Old World culture. Needless to say, the cultural involvement of the United States with Europe was complete, for culturally the United States was, until just the other day, a parasite nation. Every time an American speaks his "native" language, every time he worships in a Christian church or a Jewish temple, every time he makes a legal contract or draws a will or serves on a jury, every time he builds a Gothic cathedral or a Roman post office or a Georgian house, every time he makes a mathematical calculation or studies flora and fauna, every time he hangs a reproduction of an Old Master or listens to chamber music or reads *A Christmas Carol* to his children, he is acknowledging the persistence and power of his cultural involvement with the Old World.

Isolation is, and has always been, a myth. So is American innocence and moral superiority. It has always been difficult to take seriously the American claim to innocence, for as long as slavery persisted, the doctrine of moral superiority could not stand up to serious examination. Yet during much of the early history of the Republic, Americans were in fact not so much innocent as free from the temptations that assailed less fortunate peoples. They were immune from religious wars and from the worst excesses of militarism; they did abate the acrimony of class conflict; they were able to provide material well-being for unprecedentedly large numbers of their people.

But gradually the Old World sloughed off many of its vices and inhumanities and overcame many of its handicaps, while the New World acquired some of all of these for itself. If the relative positions of the two societies were not wholly reversed, they were, after a fashion, brought into equilibrium. Old World monarchs were no longer absolute, and in time most European governments could claim to be at least as democratic as the American. The Inquisition disappeared and so, too, religious intolerance; and if anti-Semitism lingered on in parts of Europe, racism lingered on in all of America. The lines between the classes were blurred, and heavy taxation closed the gap between the rich and the poor; but Americans developed their own version of class consciousness and dug a gulf between rich and poor as deep as any in Europe. In the more obvious tests of morality there was, on the whole, little to choose between Old World and New. Certainly the American lost whatever innocence he might once have displayed, and by the time Henry James got to *The Ambassadors* (1903), he stood on its head the theme of New World virtue and Old World corruption which he had announced in *The American* (1877) and *Daisy Miller* (1878).

It takes a long time for changes of this nature to reveal themselves and for an awareness of them to percolate down to the mind of the average American—changes in America of which he was only dimly aware, changes in Europe of which he was quite unaware. Millions who had been born to the older myths were not prepared to abandon or to reconsider them; other millions who had embraced the myth as part of the process of Americanization persisted in the conviction that they had made the right choice, and handed on that conviction to their children. So the myth of New World superiority survived and flourished long after it had served whatever purpose it may have had.

It required the agitation, the turmoil, the violence and disillusionment of the 1950s and 1960s to dramatize the anachronistic quality of these myths. In these decades blow after blow rained down upon the American consciousness, dissolved American superiority, dissipated confidence and shattered complacency. In the sixties—it can almost be dated from the assassination of President Kennedy—Americans awoke with a sense of shock and incredulity to the discovery

that the American Dream was largely an illusion. Twenty
million Negroes were second-class citizens—or worse. Thirty
million poor made a mockery of the proud claims of an
affluent society. For two hundred years Americans had laid
waste the exceeding bounty of nature, cut down the forests,
destroyed the soil, polluted the rivers and the lakes, killed
off much of the wildlife and gravely upset the balance of
nature; and now at last an outraged nature was revolting.
Cities everywhere were rotting away; crime flourished not
only on the streets but in high places; the supposed demands
of security had qualified the institutions of democracy and of
constitutionalism, and permanently shifted the balance in
the relationship of the military to the civilian power. The
nation which had invented revolution had become the most
powerful bulwark against revolution; the nation which had
fought colonialism and imperialism had become, in the eyes
of much of the world, the greatest champion of both; the
nation which Jefferson had dedicated to peace had become
the most militaristic of great powers and was waging a
pitiless war of aggression on a distant continent.

Yet notwithstanding reality, the myths of isolation and
of superiority persist; they still condition, if they do not
dominate, much of our foreign policy.

We are no longer isolated, but are connected with more
nations and organizations than any other power. We boast
military establishments in some sixty nations, and a CIA
operating in at least that number. We are an American
power whose word, we like to think, is fiat in this hemisphere. We are a European power, and NATO is not the sole
instrument of and the monument to the principle that we are
legitimately in Europe. And now we assert that we are an
Asian power.

Clearly all this is the very opposite of, and negation of,
isolation; but it is, just as clearly, a re-emergence of the

ancient notion of the uniqueness of America. For now, once again, as in the eighteenth century, we are prepared to go it alone. There are other powers, to be sure—Britain and France, for example—but they do not really count, and when the going is tough we do not bother to consult them. We did not consult them at the time of the Cuban crisis, which might have plunged them into an atomic war; we did not consult them at the time of our intervention in Vietnam, which came in defiance of the Geneva agreements. In New York City there is, to be sure, a United Nations, which we were largely responsible for setting up, but we do not take it very seriously or permit it to function in matters we consider vital to ourselves. No, we are the one true world power; we are the spokesman for the Free World; we are prepared to respond—so says our Congress—wherever freedom is threatened by communism or subversion. And that is what we have done, though not, it must be confessed, very consistently or with a very careful definition of what constitutes a threat to freedom: witness the Truman Doctrine, the Eisenhower Doctrine, the Lebanon venture, the domination of Western Germany, unilateral intervention in Latin America and unilateral intervention in Asia (for SEATO, which is designed to provide a cloak of respectability to our venture in Vietnam, is of course our creature).

And paradoxically, American power acts as American weakness once acted: to exempt us from the ordinary relationships and responsibilities that burden other nations, to encourage us to set standards to which we expect all other nations to conform.

Thus, as we have become the greatest of world powers, we have achieved a new isolation that is positive rather than negative: a moral isolation. In the first century of our history we isolated ourselves because we would not accept the moral standards of the nations of the Old World. Now we isolate ourselves because we have formulated and unilaterally apply political, military and moral stands that the nations of the Old World will not accept. Not our lack of power, but our abuse of power, has isolated us.

The second great myth—moral superiority, which sets us apart from the power-hungry nations of the Old World, with their armies, their conquests and their empires, and their disregard for the sanctity of law and of treaties—is now relied upon to justify an almost limitless exercise of power by the United States. In the past this consciousness of superiority enabled us to indulge in conduct which in other nations was odious, because our purposes were benevolent and our hearts were pure. Today it underlies and rationalizes an exercise of power in every quarter of the globe that is quite unprecedented in history. Because now, as in the past, we are confident that we represent freedom, law, order, justice and the wave of the future, we feel justified in pursuing policies of intervention, subversion and aggression which we have always judged to be reprehensible in others. We acknowledge the United Nations but assert, nevertheless, that on us alone rests ultimate responsibility for keeping the peace and for preventing aggression. We recognize the binding character of treaties, and even multiply them, but we do not in fact feel bound by them if they get in the way of saving the "free world." We are unqualifiedly dedicated to the search for peace, but carry on that search with the heaviest military arsenal that any nation ever possessed—or used. In the name of defeating "aggression" and achieving "peace" we pour onto one small country a heavier tonnage of bombs than we dropped on either Germany or Japan during the whole of the last war. We plead for the peaceful use of the atomic weapon and tremble with indignation when China detonates her own atomic bombs, but we do not choose to remember that we are, so far, the only nation that ever used atomic weapons in war; nor do we seem to find it odd that our own military and political leaders threaten to use atomic weapons again if they think the situation requires it.

It is this deeply ingrained notion of the moral superiority of the United States, and the superiority too of her institutions and her way of life, that enables us, with straight face and even with straight conscience, to maintain a double standard of morality in international relations. Thus communism is by very definition aggressive, but not capitalism: intervention in Hungary proved that, and intervention in Santo Domingo proved nothing. China is not "peace-loving" and cannot therefore be admitted to the United Nations; but we—even though we ring both the Soviet Union and China with air bases, armies and navies—are by definition "peace-loving." When Communist countries carry on clandestine activities abroad, their conduct is subversive, and indeed they are engaged in an "international conspiracy"; but when our CIA engages in clandestine activities in sixty countries, it is a legitimate branch of foreign policy. North Vietnam, when it had less than a thousand soldiers in the South, was "an aggressor nation"; but half a million American soldiers in Vietnam, the largest fleet in the world off Vietnamese waters and daily bombings of the North did not make us an aggressor nation. The Soviet Union has puppet states, and we look upon them with justified contempt; but our own puppet states—South Korea, Taiwan, Vietnam, Thailand, even, in a sense, the Philippines—are merely showing how enlightened they are when they cooperate with us. We do not permit a sovereign Cuba to invite the Soviet to establish military installations on its island; but we think it entirely proper that an independent Thailand should invite us to establish what is the world's largest airfield in their territory, and see no reason why China should take this amiss. If Russian or Chinese planes should fly over American soil we would regard that as an intolerable violation of international law; but we make daily flights over China without troubling ourselves about the law. When, in an undeclared and illegal intervention in Guatemala some twelve or thirteen years ago, we established an illegal blockade and bombed a British freighter which failed to recognize that blockade, no one supposed that Britain would retaliate by bombing New England; when, in a war in which we were not as yet involved, the North Vietnamese fired at—but did not hit—one of our cruisers escorting enemy gunboats, we made that a *casus belli* and retaliated with years of ceaseless bombardment. When, in the last war, Germans destroyed villages because they had harbored snipers, we were justly outraged; but any Vietnamese who so much as fires a gun at one of our planes invites the instant destruction of his village by our outraged airmen. We looked with horror on the concentration camps of the last war; but we set up "refugee" camps in Vietnam which are, for all practical purposes, concentration camps. And we have driven as large a proportion of the Vietnamese people from their homes, destroyed as much of their forests, their crops, their dams, their villages, as did the Germans in the Low Countries or in France in the last war.

We have long known that "power corrupts"; but we do not think that power corrupts us or can ever corrupt us, because we always wield it for the benefit of mankind.

Only a people infatuated with their own moral virtue, their own superiority, their own exemption from the ordinary laws of history and of morality, could so uncritically embrace a double standard of morality as have the American people. Only a people whose traditions of isolation have made them immune to world opinion could be surprised that they have forfeited the respect of much of mankind by their misuse of power throughout the globe.

Can We Limit
Presidential Power?

Under the skillful prodding of Senator Fulbright, the Senate Committee on Foreign Relations has recommended for adoption a resolution designed to restrain the authority of the President in the use of armed forces outside the United States. Undersecretary Katzenbach, in turn, has informed the committee that its resolution is irrelevant and futile and that the President will, in effect, recognize no limits on his conduct of foreign relations other than those imposed by his own judgment. Senator Fulbright warns us of an erosion of the congressional power which will, if not arrested, permanently alter the balance of power contrived by the framers of the Constitution; presidential spokesmen reply that the balance has already been shattered and that nothing can be done now to put it back together again.

It is an old problem, as old as Washington's Neutrality Proclamation and as recent as Secretary Rusk's refusal to commit the President to consulting the Senate about sending perhaps as many as another 200,000 troops to Vietnam. It is

First printed in *The New Republic*, April 6, 1968.

rooted in the ambiguity of the constitutional provision for the Presidency—"The executive power shall be vested in a President"—and it has not been clarified by miscellaneous Supreme Court decisions, from *Martin v. Mott* in 1828 to the Youngstown Steel decision of 1952.

The current crisis has new ingredients, not found in earlier assertions of executive authority by Monroe, Polk, Lincoln, Theodore Roosevelt and Wilson, ingredients which have enormously aggravated the familiar problem of reconciling the imperative of a strong President in the realm of foreign affairs with the constitutional arrangements for separation of powers and limitations on powers. These new ingredients go far to justify the use of such terms as "erosion" and "aggrandizement."

First, unlimited executive power in foreign relations and war is no longer justified as emergency but as normal and almost routine. In raising armies without congressional sanction, in the suspension of the *habeas corpus,* in the Emancipation Proclamation, Lincoln pushed his powers to the outward limits of what was constitutionally permissible; but he said, with humility, that the emergency required him to do this and that Congress would doubtless give retroactive approval to what he had done. No such humility characterized what we may call the Johnson-Katzenbach theory of executive authority.

Second, our current presidential commitments are global rather than, as with Lincoln, domestic, or as with Polk, Cleveland and Wilson, limited to the Western hemisphere and rationalized, or justified, by the Monroe Doctrine.

Third, the new executive commitments are not, as commonly in the past, *ad hoc* and practical, but general and ideological. We do not now take arms because "American blood has been shed on American soil," nor does the President respond to an inescapable emergency such as the attack on Fort Sumter. Now our President acts to "contain communism," to frustrate an "international conspiracy," to protect something vaguely called "vital interests" in far corners of the globe. Thus Secretary Rusk's notorious assertion of 1966 that "no would-be aggressor should suppose that the absence of a defense treaty, congressional declaration, or United States military presence, grants immunity to aggression." The key words are, of course, "absence of treaty" and "congressional declaration."

Fourth, for the first time in our history we are members of an international organization which is responsible for preserving the peace and arbitrating dangerous controversies; indeed, in a sense it is *our* organization, imagined by Woodrow Wilson, brought into being by Franklin Roosevelt. Yet our formal declarations of what the President is prepared to do throughout the globe (and, it must be confessed, declarations of what the Congress is prepared to support) effectively bypass the United Nations. There are occasional gestures toward involving the United Nations in the war in Vietnam, but these are indeed gestures rather than genuine efforts. Certainly we did not even pretend to invoke or involve the UN in our original attack on North Vietnam, nor, for that matter, in our adventures in Guatemala, Cuba and Santo Domingo, nor did we even involve the Organization of American States in these ventures until we could confront it with a *fait accompli*. And whatever might have been said for the conduct of a Polk or a Theodore Roosevelt in justification of unilateral action can no longer be said for the conduct of President Johnson, for we are committed now, as we were not earlier, to procedures established by the UN Charter and by the Organization of American States.

A fifth new ingredient is philosophically as ancient as the precept that power corrupts. It is that the possession of power encourages and even creates conditions which seem to require its use, and that the greater and more conclusive the power the stronger the argument for its use. Those who possess authority want to exercise it: children, teachers, bosses, bureaucrats, even soldiers and statesmen. Just the other day General Mark Clark, speaking with exquisite appropriateness at a memorial service for a leading Catholic churchman, argued that if the going got tough in Vietnam we should not hesitate to use "tactical" nuclear weapons. Men who possess power think it a shame to let power go to waste, and sometimes, perhaps unconsciously, they manufacture situations in which it must be used—as in Santo Domingo, for example. All this was dangerous but not intolerable in the pre-atomic age; it is no longer tolerable.

The problem of the unauthorized use of the executive power in situations that might result in war is complicated by the obsolescence of old and conventional terminology. Thus the once traditional argument that, in his capacity of Commander in Chief, the President is authorized to take "defensive" but not "offensive" action has little meaning today, for now all military action is defensive. Even Hitler claimed that his assault on Poland was "defensive." That we ourselves are not backward is clear from the wording of the Tonkin Gulf resolution that "the Congress approves and supports the determination of the President to repel armed attack . . . and to prevent further aggression." You could not hope to have a clearer statement of the purely defensive nature of this war than that, nor a more alarming picture of the aggression which President Johnson is now heroically resisting.

So too with the once fairly simple notion of what is national territory or what are territorial waters. It was Franklin Roosevelt, after all, who said that the American frontier was on the Rhine, and Roosevelt too who officially extended American territorial waters 300 miles off the Atlantic coast. What would our government say today if China should adopt the Roosevelt principle that her territorial waters extend 300 miles out from her coast, and if she should issue a "shoot at sight" order to Chinese ships?

Or there is the relatively new concept of "vital interests" —a concept with no standing in international law and no understanding even in politics. When in 1957 Congress authorized President Eisenhower to protect the "vital interests" of the United States in the Middle East, the President in effect repudiated that particular justification, and dispatched 14,000 American soldiers to Lebanon "to protect American lives and property." But "vital interest" has now become the official rationale of our presence in Vietnam. What that vital interest is, or what our interest in Vietnam is vital to, remains opaque.

It is not only concepts like "defensive" and "offensive" warfare, or "vital interests" or "territorial waters" that are outmoded; Undersecretary Katzenbach formally asserted to the Senate Foreign Relations Committee that declarations of war are equally outmoded, thus neatly repealing a clause in the Constitution without the bother of congressional and state action. The Tonkin Gulf resolution—which senators now say they did not understand—together with the SEATO treaty, which no one understands, constitute, said Mr. Katzenbach, the "functional equivalent to a declaration of war."

The argument for latitude in the exercise of presidential power draws great strength from a recognition that in a nuclear age emergencies may require instantaneous action. Four times in the past seven years Presidents have mounted major military interventions without congressional authority, on the plea of emergency: the Bay of Pigs, the missile crisis, Santo Domingo, and Vietnam. Only one of these—the missile crisis—could claim to be a genuine emergency, and, in a larger sense, even this was an emergency of our own making, for it is arguable that the whole Cuban muddle was a product of our miscalculations about Batista and Castro. If the Bay of Pigs situation and the Santo Domingo election dispute represented emergencies so imperative that there was no time to consult Congress, then anything whatsoever can be twisted into an emergency and the traditional requirement of consultation with the Congress is a thing of the past.

Can anything, then, be done to protect the use but avoid the misuse of presidential powers?

Not, it must be confessed, very much.

There are, of course, obvious and official solutions. The Senate might repeal the Tonkin Gulf resolutions; the House might cut off appropriations; Congress might impeach the President. (When Senator Fulbright merely listed this as one of the constitutional safeguards he was resoundingly rebuked by Senator Lausche, who apparently thought the Constitution un-American!)

None of these remedies is available. The Senate is quite as belligerent as the President; the House has never yet refused appropriations to conduct a war; no President has been removed from office. Furthermore, if the Congress did try to restrain the President in the conduct of war he could as Commander in Chief still commit troops—as indeed President Johnson has done in both Vietnam and Santo Domingo —or he could act in secrecy, as President Kennedy did at the time of the missile crisis, and present the nation with a *fait accompli*. Furthermore, public opinion almost always supports the President against Congress, and is against anything that can be called "retreat" or "surrender." Even if public opinion should turn against President Johnson, there is little chance of any change of policy, for has he not himself said that if his support (in the polls!) should drop to one percent he would still persist in his program?

Can the Fulbright resolution do what other constitutional and political restrictions have failed to do?

"It is the sense of the Senate," so reads the resolution,

"that a national commitment by the United States to a foreign power, necessarily and exclusively results from affirmative action taken by the executive and legislative branches of the United States government through means of a treaty, convention or other legislative instrumentality specifically intended to give effect to such commitment."

Admirable as it is, this resolution holds out little hope of effectiveness. If it had been on the statute books at the time of the Tonkin Gulf episode or at the inception of our bombing of North Vietnam, would it have prevented or mitigated these actions? Surely not, for the administration would have cited—as it does tirelessly—the "obligations" of the SEATO treaty, or it would have invoked the amorphous concept of "vital interest."

Would the resolution have avoided the Cuban missile crisis? No, because action at that time was not alleged to be based on a national "commitment" but on presidential responsibility to defend the United States against attack.

Would it have stayed Eisenhower's interventions in Lebanon or in the Pescadores? No, because these had Senate endorsement after a fashion. Would it have avoided intervention in Guatemala in the early fifties, or the more notorious intervention in Santo Domingo in 1965? Probably not, for intervention in Santo Domingo—like that in Lebanon—was justified on the argument that American lives were in peril, while our Guatemalan adventure was so private that to this day the Congress seems unacquainted with it.

Are there, then, any practical measures that we might devise that would have any likelihood of adoption by the Congress and acceptance by the President—two very different things?

The Senate might give effect to the constitutional provisions for participating in the conduct of foreign affairs by providing that the Foreign Relations Committee, or a quorum of it, should remain permanently in Washington, instructed to consult with the President on any matter of foreign policy thought important.

Would the President in fact consult with the committee? Secretary Rusk's evidence before that committee makes this prospect highly improbable.

An entirely different approach suggests itself only to retreat in confusion: that the United States take seriously its obligations under the United Nations, and invoke, and abide by, decisions of the UN on all controversies in which it is involved. How much easier and safer if our President would hand over to the UN the difficult problems of Guatemala, Santo Domingo, Lebanon, Vietnam, Cuba, and now Korea. There is no reason in law, or in logic, why this could not happen; the reasons why it does not, and will not, happen are political and psychological.

These proposals, like that of the Fulbright committee, or Professor Carl Kaysen's proposal that no money appropriated by Congress might be used to support soldiers outside the continental United States without prior approval by the Congress, offer little likelihood of effective restraint.

Where, then, do we turn?

When there is no response to "What is the answer?" it is useful to ask "What is the question?" Perhaps here, as elsewhere, we are asking the wrong question. If there are no solutions to this intransigent problem of the abuse of presidential power, we will do well to go back and start over again and reconsider the nature of the problem itself.

If we consider those exercises of presidential power in the past two decades which bypassed the Congress—and perhaps the Constitution; if we contemplate the Truman Doctrine, the Korean war, the Pescadores crisis, the Laotian imbroglio, participation in the Vietnam war even before 1956, the Lebanon doctrine, intervention in Guatemala, Santo Domingo and Cuba, the missile crisis, the activities of the CIA in some sixty countries, large-scale intervention in Vietnam and

Thailand, and the newly erupted quarrel with North Korea —we detect that they have one common denominator. All are inspired by and directed to Communist threats, real or imagined. All are skirmishes or battles in the cold war. All are functions of our obsession with communism and of our notion that we have been chosen by providence to contain communism everywhere on the globe. Furthermore, almost all of the attitudes and gestures which distinguish the current claims for the outmost reach of the presidential power have, on closer examination, the same common denominator: namely, that when a threat of Communist conspiracy or Communist subversion is implicit or explicit in any situation, no limit can be or will be put on the executive power necessary to dispose of that threat.

If the pattern is clear, so too is its meaning. Until we can rid ourselves of our delusions of universalism and our obsessions with communism and other ideological threats— which are, in last analysis, the inspiration for our war in Vietnam—we will not and cannot abate presidential abuse of power in foreign affairs.

The misuse of executive power where communism is, or appears to be, involved is not a phenomenon of the Presidency or of individual Presidents. After all, when we trace a harmonious pattern of the use of the executive power in Franklin Roosevelt, Truman, Eisenhower, Kennedy and Johnson, we are forced to conclude that what we have is not a manifestation of personal or even official ambition but something inherent in the Presidency and in the age in which these Presidents serve.

Nor have Presidents been alone, or even idiosyncratic, in their illusions about total power, or in their obsessions with communism. If they were, that would indeed be cause to tremble for the republic, for then it might be said that the fears of the Founding Fathers about the innate corruption of men in power were about to be realized. But presidential advisers, from Acheson to Rostow, share these obsessions; congressmen declaim them; a substantial segment of the American people confess them.

The creation of this national paranoia is a responsibility which almost all of us share: political parties and leaders, the press, the church, the school and the Academy. And as most, or all, of these have some responsibility for creating or permitting the situation which now provides the logic for the abuse of presidential powers, all share responsibility for re-educating Presidents, congressmen, editors, and the American people about the dangers implicit in the arrogance of power and the danger of ideological obsessions. Until the forces, motives and fears which underlie the exercise and the rationale of excessive presidential power are dissipated we will not abate that power.

This is a hard job and may be an impossible one. But is it really harder to wean the American people from their obsessions and educate them to the realities of world politics than it is to cut back on presidential powers by constitutional or political means?

Abuse of power by Presidents is a reflection, and perhaps a consequence, of abuse of power by the American people and nation. For almost two decades now we have misused our vast power. We misused our economic power, not least in associating economic with military assistance and military with economic support, and in imposing economic sanctions against nations who did not see eye to eye with us about trade with our "enemies." We misused our political power by trying to force neutrals onto our side in the cold war and by bringing pressure on the nations of Latin America to support our shortsighted policy of excluding China from the United Nations. We have grossly misused our political power—if it may be called that—by planting the CIA in some sixty countries to carry on its work of subversion. We have misused our military power in forcing our weapons on scores of nations around the globe, maintaining our military organizations and alliances like NATO and SEATO—the first of which has outlived its usefulness, the second of which never had any usefulness to begin with. And we are now engaged in a monstrous misuse of power in waging war on a distant people who do not accept our ideology. We have even misused our moral power by bringing pressure on former allies and associates to join us in the cold war against the Soviet Union and China; and history may yet find the United States chiefly responsible for exacerbating the disunity of Germany and the division between East and West by exploiting Germany for cold-war purposes. That seems to be the de Gaulle interpretation of our role in Europe, and de Gaulle is more often right than wrong.

As we have greater power than any other nation, so we should display greater moderation in using it and greater humility in justifying it. We display neither moderation nor humility, but immoderation and that arrogance of power which Senator Fulbright has so eloquently denounced.

In the long run, then, the abuse of the executive power cannot be separated from the abuse of national power. If we subvert world order and destroy world peace, we must inevitably subvert and destroy our own political institutions first. This we are now in the process of doing.

Determining
on Peace and War

In the historic steel-seizure case of 1952 Justice Jackson said, "What is at stake is the equilibrium of our constitutional system." Now, after twenty years marked by repeated and almost routine invasions by the executive of the war-making powers assigned by the Constitution to Congress, we can see that more is at stake than the constitutional principle of the separation of powers. At stake is the fate of the age-long effort of men to fix effective limits on government; at stake, the reconciliation of the claims of freedom and of security; at stake, the fateful issue of peace or war, an issue fateful not for the American people alone, nor alone for the stricken peoples of Southeast Asia, but for the whole of mankind.

Five times in the past ten years Presidents have mounted major military interventions in foreign nations without prior consultation with the Congress: the Bay of Pigs, the invasion of the Dominican Republic and the attacks on North

Statement delivered before U. S. Senate, Committee on Foreign Relations, March 8, 1971.

Vietnam, Cambodia, and Laos. None of these now appears to have represented a genuine emergency; none was in response to an attack upon the United States which implacably required immediate military reaction. None therefore appears to meet the requirements for the exercise of war powers by the President formulated by the makers of the Constitution.

The Constitution, as written in 1787 and as developed over a century and three-quarters, is of course a product of history, not the conclusion of a syllogism, and any consideration of the war powers must be rooted in history rather than in theory.

There is no ambiguity about the intent of the framers of the Constitution. They proposed to make it impossible for a "ruler" to plunge the nation into war. In the Old World monarchs had "the sole prerogative of making war and peace"—the phrase is from Blackstone's *Commentaries*—and the Founding Fathers were determined that no American executive would have the power of a George II or a Frederick the Great. To that end too they provided a fairly rigid separation of powers. This also was something new in history, for while philosophers of the Old World recognized a "balance" of powers, none had imagined the kind of functional separation which Americans established in their state and national constitutions. Separation of powers, as Justice Brandeis observed in a now classic *obiter dictum,* "was adopted by the Convention of 1787 not to promote efficiency but to preclude the exercise of arbitrary power. The purpose was not to avoid friction, but by means of the inevitable friction incident to the distribution of the governmental powers among three departments, to save the people from autocracy" (*Myers v. U.S., 272 U.S.* at 293).

Experience under the Articles of Confederation throws only a flickering of light on our problem, for there was in fact no proper executive in the confederation. It was inevitable, therefore, that the Articles of Confederation assigned to the Congress "the sole and exclusive right and power to determining on peace and war." A good phrase that, "determining on war"; a pity we did not retain it. Something is to be drawn from the relation of Congress to the Commander in Chief. Suffice it to note—as casting some light on the meaning that the Constitution makers infused into the phrase—that Washington's commission required him "punctually to observe and follow such orders and directions from time to time as he shall receive from this and future Congresses," because—we can assert this with confidence—everyone, including Washington himself, took for granted the supremacy of the civil over the military power and took for granted that the term "Commander in Chief" described not another Louis XIV or Frederick or George but a Washington. How revealing that even Hamilton, always ardent for power, provided in his famous draft constitution that the President was to be Commander in Chief and "to have the direction of the war *when authorized or begun.*" (Note in another version of speech, "the direction of war *when commenced*" [I Farrand 292 and III Farrand 624]. This limited view of the powers of the Commander in Chief persisted almost down to our own time. As late as 1940 Attorney General Robert Jackson could inform the President, "Happily there has been little occasion in our history for the interpretation of powers of the President as Commander in Chief of the Army and Navy"; and he added that he did not base on that phrase justification for the destroyer-bases agreement with Britain.

The Constitution makers proposed to assign to the legislature the power to declare war—e.g., to decide on war—and to the executive the power to make or conduct or direct the war. This is inescapably clear from the all-too-brief discussion of these words and phrases in the convention; it is sufficient to note here what is familiar enough: that the shift in terms from "make" to "declare" was designed to preserve to "the executive the power to repel sudden attacks." Roger Sherman wanted to nail that down: the President "should be able to repel *and not to commence war.*" And as for the always cautious George Mason of Virginia, "He was against giving the power of war to the executive because he was not to be trusted with it. . . . He was for clogging, not for facilitating, the making of war."

Hamilton took it upon himself to explain the presidential powers in the *Federalist Papers.* In No. 69 he wrote that the authority of the President as Commander in Chief "would amount to nothing more than the supreme command and direction of the military and naval forces, as first general and admiral of the confederacy." In No. 74 he returned to the point. "The direction of war," he wrote, "implies the direction of the common strength, and the power of directing and employing the common strength forms an essential part of the executive authority." No. 75 is a bit more sweeping:

> The history of human conduct does not warrant that exalted opinion of human virtue which would make it wise in a nation to commit interests of so delicate and momentous a kind as those which concern its intercourse with the rest of the world to the sole disposal of a magistrate created and circumstanced as would be a President of the United States.

And a decade later, even as he argued the propriety of presidential response to the threat of the Barbary corsairs, he once again indicated the accepted limits of executive power in this realm: "It is the peculiar and exclusive province of Congress, when the nation is at peace, to change that to a state of war . . ." In other worlds, *it belongs to Congress only to go to war.*

But it is Madison, not Hamilton, who has a just claim

to be considered not only the father of the Constitution but its most authoritative interpreter. Writing as Helvidius, in 1793, he addressed himself to precisely this problem of executive power to make war:

> Every just view that can be taken of this subject admonishes the public of the necessity of a rigid adherence to the simple, the received, and the fundamental doctrine of the Constitution, that the power to declare war including the power of judging the causes of war, is *fully and exclusively vested in the legislature,* that the executive has no right in any case, to decide the question whether there is or is not cause for declaring war, that the right of convening and informing Congress whenever such a question seems to call for a decision, is all the right which the Constitution has deemed requisite or proper. (*Works of James Madison,* Hunt, ed. VI, 174)

And he added an observation which we may take to heart today: "In no part of the Constitution is more wisdom to be found than in the clause which confines the question of war or peace to the legislature and not to the executive department."

It is fair to say that those statesmen who were closest to the Constitution makers—the statesmen of the generation of the Founding Fathers and their successors—seemed all but unanimous in this interpretation of the war powers. Here is Jefferson reporting to Congress on the decision to defend American ships against the Barbary corsairs:

> The bravery exhibited by our citizens on that element [the sea] will be a testimony to the world that it is not the want of that virtue which makes us seek their peace, but a conscientious desire to direct the energies of our nation to the multiplication of the human race,

not to its destruction. . . . Unauthorized by the Constitution, without the sanction of Congress, to go beyond the line of defense, the vessel, being disabled from committing further hostilities, was liberated. The legislature will doubtless consider whether by authorizing measures of defense also, they will place our force on an equal footing.

Or here is John Quincy Adams, surely one of the most learned of constitutional lawyers, speaking to the problem of dealing with a threat from the Holy Alliance—a threat surely more serious than the alleged threat from China in our own time:

> With respect to the question, in what manner the government of the United States intends to resist on its part any interference of the Holy Alliance for the purpose of subjugating the new republics . . . you understand that by the Constitution of the United States the ultimate decision of this question belongs to the legislative department of the government.

Or Daniel Webster—who knew something of the Constitution and championed the presidential power—writing in 1851, as Secretary of State, on the proposal to intervene in Hawaii:

> In the first place I have to say that the war-making power in this government rests entirely with Congress, and that the President can authorize belligerent operations only in the cases expressly provided for by the Constitution and the laws. By these no power is given to the executive to oppose an attack by one independent nation on the possessions of another. . . . If this interference be an act of hostile force, it is not within the constitutional power of the President.

And finally consider how Secretary of State Lewis Cass disposed of a proposal that the United States intervene in China over a century ago:

This proposition [he wrote in 1857 to Lord Napier] looking to a participation by the United States in the existing hostilities against China makes it proper to remind your Lordship that, under the Constitution of the United States, the executive branch of this government is not the war-making power. The exercise of that great attribute of sovereignty is vested in Congress, and the President has no authority to order aggressive hostilities to be undertaken.

Needless to say, presidential conduct did not always correspond with presidential principles, and the correspondence grew—let us not say more tenuous but more fortuitous—with the passing of time. It is not necessary to detail here the many examples of executive use or abuse of war powers.

In 1818 President Monroe authorized General Jackson to engage in "hot pursuit" of the Seminole Indians into Spanish Florida: always eager to smite the enemy, Jackson showed perhaps excessive zeal, captured Spanish forts and hanged Arbuthnot and Ambrister, two British subjects.

In 1845 President Polk ordered General Scott to occupy the disputed land between the Nueces and the Rio Grande rivers; when the Mexicans advanced into the territory he engaged in battle—purely on presidential authority. "American blood has been shed on American soil," Polk announced, and only then asked for congressional authority to fight. Polk earned the name "Polk the Mendacious," but public opinion rejoiced in the fruits of the war.

In 1854 President Pierce authorized the bombardment of the city of Greytown, on the Mosquito Coast; and that act of quasi war rested exclusively on presidential fiat. President Lincoln raised armies, launched campaigns, declared a blockade and suspended the writ of *habeas corpus* all on his own. More clearly than other executives who invoked the war powers, he was able to fall back upon the constitutional obligation to see that the laws were faithfully executed. And we are still debating the thorny question whether the Civil War was a war within the meaning of the Constitution or not; certainly there was no declaration of war or a treaty of peace, nor was there a "foreign" enemy. Grant's escapade in Santo Domingo in 1869 is notorious—and was embarrassing. McKinley launched an expeditionary force of 5,000 men into China—part of the Boxer expedition —without bothering to obtain congressional approval: a fateful precedent. Theodore Roosevelt's interventions in the Caribbean—like those, later, of Taft, Wilson, and Coolidge —were mostly without benefit of congressional authorization. Wilson ordered the bombardment of Vera Cruz on his own, and so too the invasion of Mexico in pursuit of the elusive Pancho Villa, though here he went through the form of getting approval from President Carranza of Mexico— an approval that speedily changed to disapproval.

It is all pretty impressive when summed up in this fashion. But it is relevant to note that in almost every instance in the nineteenth century, and in most of the first half of the twentieth, presidential intervention was confined to the western hemisphere and even to contiguous territory or our *mare nostrum*, the Caribbean. President McKinley's astonishing participation in the Boxer expedition came, with a symbolic appropriateness, in the year 1900. Yet even Franklin Roosevelt's executive agreements with Britain for a destroyer-bases exchange and with Denmark for the occupation of Iceland and Greenland, which pushed what was permissible to the furthest extreme, could be held, not implausibly, to be a legitimate part of hemispheric defense.

It is only in the last twenty years or so that Presidents appear to have thrown caution and even constitutional scruples to the winds, as it were, and ventured on their own authority into military operations that were in fact acts of war, that were on a large scale, that were in distant parts of the globe, and that constituted "commitments" whose vindication threatened the integrity of our political and constitutional system.

It is not sufficiently realized that the kind of intervention we have witnessed in the past quarter century is, if not wholly unprecedented, clearly a departure from a long and deeply rooted tradition. Since the Neutrality Proclamation of 1793, that tradition has been one of nonintervention, not intervention. Washington, and his Cabinet, refused to intervene in the wars between France and her enemies even though the United States was far more deeply "committed" to come to the aid of France by the terms of the treaty of alliance of 1778 than she was to intervene in Vietnam by the terms of the SEATO treaty. Notwithstanding almost universal sympathy for the peoples of Latin America who sought to throw off Spanish rule, we did not intervene militarily in that conflict. The ideas of manifest destiny and "young America" dictated support to peoples everywhere struggling to throw off ancient tyrannies, but no President intervened militarily in the Greek struggle for independence from Turkey, the Italian uprisings against Austria, the Hungarian revolution of 1848, or other internal revolutions of that fateful year, Garibaldi's fight for Italian independence, the many Irish uprisings against Britain, in Ireland and in Canada—close to home, that—or even, *mirabile dictu*, the ten-year war of the Cubans against their Spanish overlords from 1868 to 1878. Nor, in more modern times, did Presidents see fit to intervene on behalf of Jewish victims of pogroms, Turkish genocide against Armenians, or Franco's overthrow of the Loyalist regime in Spain. Whether such abstention was always wise is a question we need not raise here. The point is that in none of these situations did the executive think it proper, or legal, to use his powers as Commander in Chief or as chief organ of foreign relations to commit the United States to military intervention in distant lands. With the sole exception of McKinley's unnecessary participation in the Boxer expedition, that concept of executive powers belongs to the past quarter century. And if it should be asked why the United States should refrain from intervention in the internal struggles of other nations, even when her sympathies are deeply involved and her interests enlisted, it is perhaps sufficient to say that few of us would be prepared to endorse a principle which would have justified the intervention of Britain and France in the American Civil War—on behalf of the Confederacy, of course—and that in international law you cannot really have it both ways.

Clearly the present crisis is a continuation of a long series of crises stretching from Washington's Proclamation of Neutrality to Truman's use of military and naval force in Korea and our current involvement in Southeast Asia. There are, however, new ingredients in the executive use of the war power which make earlier precedents if not irrelevant then far from conclusive and which greatly enhance the threat to the integrity of our constitutional system and to the peace of the world. Let me deal briefly with these.

First, our current presidential commitments—and if we cannot curb these, our future as well—are global rather than, as with Lincoln, domestic, or as with Monroe, Polk, Roosevelt and Wilson, hemispheric. They are not to be justified by invoking the Monroe Doctrine or its accumulated corollaries; they are justified rather by new doctrines such as that of "vital interest" or by the "Nixon doctrine" of shared responsibility. Of both of these it can be said that their most conspicuous feature is the fog which enshrouds them.

Second, the umlimited power of the executive in foreign relations is no longer justified as an emergency power, but is asserted to be a normal and almost routine exercise of executive authority. Lincoln pushed his authority to the outward limits of what was constitutionally permissible, but confessed, with characteristic humility, that the emergency required him to do what he did, and asked Congress to give retroactive sanction to his acts. No such humility characterizes what we may call the Johnson-Nixon theory of executive authority. Thus President Johnson asserted that he did not need the authority of the Tonkin Gulf resolution to justify his bombardment of North Vietnam, for he already had that; thus President Nixon's Assistant Attorney General, Richard Kleindienst, asserted that the President's authority to invade Cambodia "*must* be conceded by even those who read executive authority narrowly" (June 16, 1970). Why *must* it be? Certainly not because of the persuasive character of the arguments advanced by distinguished counsel, for that character—as that distinction—is wanting.

Third, the new commitments are not, as generally in the past, *ad hoc* and even fortuitous, but calculated and ideological. Thus we did not drop bombs on Vietnam or Laos because "American blood has been shed on American soil"—Polk's excuse; nor did the President respond to an imperative like the attack of Fort Sumter or even to U-boat warfare; nor did recent Presidents presume to act—like President Truman—in response to a United Nations decision. Now Presidents act to "contain communism" or to protect "vital interests" 9,000 miles away, or to fulfull "commitments" that are somehow never made clear and that other nations pledged to them just as solemnly, somehow do not think require military fulfullment (e.g., the SEATO "commitments" which bind Britain, France, and Pakistan)—and they do so by programs which are by their very nature open-ended and tenacious. Thus Secretary Rusk's assertion in 1966 that "no would-be aggressor should suppose that the absence of a defense treaty, congressional declaration, or United States military presence, grants immunity to aggression." The key words for our purposes are "absence of treaty" and "absence of congressional declaration," for this left only the alternative of the application of the executive power, unilaterally in the international arena, unilaterally in the United States constitutional arena too.

Fourth, we are a charter member of the United Nations, whose function it is to settle international disputes peacefully. Yet presidential declarations of what they are prepared to do around the globe blatantly bypass the United Nations and the International Court of Justice, and thus add to the undermining of our own Constitution the undermining of the United Nations.

Fifth, as power corrupts, the possession of great power encourages and even creates conditions in which it seems imperative to use it, and the concentration of that power vastly increases the risks of misuse. We had one example of that as early as 1846. What began as a simple vindication of a boundary line ended up as a war in which we tore Mexico in two.

Now, the original assumption of our Constitution-framers, that a President might not engage in war on his own, was greatly strengthened by the elementary fact that he could not if he wanted to, because there were no armies or navies with which to conduct war. At the time of the ratification of the Constitution the United States Army consisted of 719 officers and men—not a formidable force for military adventures. The situation did not change perceptibly over the years. Our armed forces increased to some 20,000 by 1840, to 28,000 on the eve of the Civil War, and to 38,000 by 1890. Even in 1915, with the world locked in mortal combat, the armed forces of the United States numbered fewer than 175,000. With the worst will, there was little that Presidents could do with these forces, little that would involve us in the kind of embroilments in which we have found ourselves in the past quarter-century.

Now we have a wholly new situation. Not only do we keep some three million men under arms at all times—since 1951 the number has rarely fallen below that—but we have the greatest and most formidable armaments that any nation ever commanded. What this means is quite simply that while in the past Presidents could not involve the nation, or the world, very deeply in war without congressional approval, now they can—and do.

The symbol of our new power is the nuclear weapon. Doubtless the threat of nuclear war goes far to justify giving the executive whatever discretion is necessary to secure survival in the face of attack. Correspondingly, our possession of the most formidable nuclear armaments places upon us a graver responsibility than we had to observe in the past. We should therefore make it our first objective to minimize the risk of a nuclear showdown. This we are not doing. As for chemical and biological warfare, it is notorious that we have used chemical defoliants; and that only a public outcry and congressional protest brought some modification of the use of chemicals and the adoption of new policies for the disposition of nerve gases.

These are new ingredients within the matrix of the presidential power, and they change the constitutional mix —for the Constitution, after all, is not static but dynamic. Thus it is conceded that the President has authority to "repel" attacks, but the term has been drained of meaning —certainly drained of the meaning that a Madison or a Jefferson read into it. When we launch invasions of Cambodia and Laos, not to defeat the enemy or to conquer territory but to enable us to "withdraw," anything can be called a protective reaction. Besides, it is a truism now that all wars are defensive. Hitler claimed that his assaults on Denmark and Norway were "defensive"; and the Tonkin Bay resolution, too, is phrased in this vocabulary, and no wonder—it was drafted in the White House. It declares that the Congress approves and supports the determination of the President "to repel armed attack against the forces of the United States and to prevent further aggression." This is as good an example as any of the "aggressions" against the United States which the President is called upon to resist!

Or there is the relatively new concept of "vital interests." In 1957 the Congress authorized President Eisenhower to protect the "vital interests" of the United States in the Middle East. It is not without interest that President Eisenhower modified that authorization and justified the dispatch of 14,000 marines to Lebanon on the principle of protecting American "lives"—very old-fashioned of him. What, after all, is a vital interest? Who, or what branch, of the government is authorized to define it and to determine when it needs protection? The parallel between the vital interest in international law and the police power in municipal law comes to mind. But the police power is always subject to review by the courts; what comparable check is there on the misuse of presidential power on behalf of what the President may consider vital interests?

It is not only concepts such as offensive and defensive war, or territorial waters, or vital interests that have been drained of their historic meaning. Even the constitutional concept of a declaration of war has been hopelessly impaired by the presidential interpretation of the Tonkin Bay resolution. Thus, in testimony to the Senate Committee on Foreign Relations in 1967, Undersecretary Katzenbach formally asserted that the Tonkin Bay resolution, together with the SEATO treaty, constituted a "functional declaration of war"—thereby combining an original contribution to international law with a repeal of an important provision of the Constitution.

There is a final consideration of vital importance: the growing role of the executive agreement as a method for bypassing the requirements of treaty-making. Unknown to Article 11 of the Constitution, the executive agreement emerged early as a useful method of disposing of routine business that did not warrant the dignity of a treaty. Until very recent times it was customarily used only for such routine business proceedings as tariff agreements, postal conventions, patent arrangements, and so forth—and the great majority of these were negotiated in pursuance of congressional authorization. As late as 1930 the United States concluded 25 treaties and only 9 executive agreements. But in 1968 it concluded 16 treaties and 266 executive agreements. As of January 1, 1969, the United States had a total of 909 treaties and 3,973 executive agreements. And while the great majority of these were still concerned with routine matters, a substantial number of them dealt with problems which in the past had been considered proper subjects of the treaty-making power. Well might the distinguished senator from Arkansas say at that time that "during the course of years . . . the Senate has allowed an imbalance to arise within our governmental structure and, by a process of acceptance of executive action, some of the most significant powers of the Senate have been lost. . . . the traditional distinction between the treaty as the appropriate means of making significant political commitments and the executive department as the appropriate instrument for routine, non-political arrangements, has substantially broken down." It cannot be said that this development came without warning. As late as 1940 Mr. Hackworth, the legal counselor to the Department of State, asserted that "from the point of view of international law, treaties and executive agreements are alike in that both constitute equally binding obligations upon the nation." He did however add a caution that has been forgotten by recent administrations, that "international agreements involving political issues or changes of national policy and those involving international arrangements of a permanent character, usually take the form of treaties." No longer.

That same year, 1940, Attorney General Jackson—later Justice of the Supreme Court—spelled out with customary clarity the permissible and impermissible limits of the use of executive agreements in foreign affairs: "The President's power over foreign relations, while delicate, plenary and exclusive, is not unlimited. Some negotiations involve commitments as to the future which would carry an obligation to exercise powers vested in the Congress. Such presidential arrangements are customarily submitted for ratification . . . of the Senate before the future legislative power of the country is committed." And he made a distinction between what was proper and what was improper relevant to the current scene: "The transaction now proposed represents only an exchange with no statutory requirements for the embodiment thereof in any treaty and involving no promises or undertakings by the United States that might raise the question of the propriety of incorporation in a treaty." It is superfluous to point out that the use of executive agreements in such areas as joint use of air bases and joint defense of them in Spain repudiates these carefully drawn limitations by Mr. Hackworth and by Justice Jackson. For these and similar agreements do, in fact, carry promises and undertakings of future action. They are properly the subject for treaties; they are not properly the subject of executive agreements.

It is impossible to escape the conclusion that the executive is whittling away the constitutional authority of the Congress in the momentous arena of treaty-making, as it is whittling away its constitutional authority in the realm of war-making.

It is a mistake, however, to concentrate exclusively on the constitutional and legal aspects of this great problem of the power to commit the nation to war. One of the dangers of our American system, against which we must be constantly alert, is the temptation to evaluate momentous questions of public policy not so much on their merits as on their legality. It is one price we pay for judicial review, and everything it implies, that as we tend to equate what is unconstitutional with what is pernicious, so we tend to equate what has a claim to constitutional correctness as thereby sound. These things are not always the same.

Besides, however we may balance the constitutional and legal arguments on the presidential power, it is highly improbable that those who have already made up their minds on the wisdom or error of our involvement in Indochina are going to be persuaded or dissuaded by merely legal arguments. Those familiar with the arguments of State Department spokesmen, witnesses before Senate committees, and law professors and others learned in the law know how easy it is to construct impressive monuments out of the *disjecta membra* of legal precedents and judicial citations. Each of us can say of the arguments of our critics and opponents what Finley Peter Dunne said of the arguments of lawyers: "What looks like a stone wall to a layman is a triumphant arch to a corporation lawyer."

Great questions of constitutional law are great not because they are complicated legal or technical questions but because they embody issues of high policy, of public good, of morality. We must consider the problem of the presidential authority to make war not merely in the light of constitutional precedents but in the light of wisdom and justice.

Let us turn from the legal and constitutional considerations to more persuasive considerations—considerations, perhaps, of historical experience, experience not as precedents but as—in the famous words of Lord Bolingbroke—"philosophy teaching by examples."

In 1967 Undersecretary Nicholas Katzenbach assured this committee that "history has surely vindicated the wisdom of the flexibility of the conduct of our foreign affairs." Two years later the distinguished senator from Wyoming, Gale McGee, stated that "the decision-making process may be reduced by events to a single day, or even hours. On more than one occasion the time allotted by crisis incidents to those who must make the decisions has been less than the time it would take to assemble a quorum of the Congress."

We must face squarely the issues raised by Mr. Katzenbach and Senator McGee: that, after all, history has vindicated the use of the presidential powers in the realm of war-making and that time has been and is of the essence. Has history in fact vindicated the use of armed forces by Presidents? Have Presidents been well advised—again in the light of history—to bypass Congress in using American armed forces overseas? Would consultation with the Congress, would even second thoughts have made a difference detrimental to national, or world, interests?

I need not rehearse the long list of episodes here but will comment on them in passing. Was it really of vital importance that General Jackson pursue the Seminoles and hang Arbuthnot and Ambrister? Would the fate of Texas have been different had Polk consulted the Congress before launching a war? Had he done so, he might have escaped the name which has clung to him through history—"Polk

the Mendacious." Was it really essential to bombard Greytown in 1854? Would we do that now? Grant himself learned
what a mistake it was to send troops to the Dominican
Republic in 1868, for a Senate, perhaps more strong-minded
than some later Senates, refused to back him up or to allow
him to go through with his plans for annexation. Was
McKinley wise to commit 5,000 troops to the invasion of
China in 1900, and would we do this today in a comparable
situation? Our commitment to the provisions of the constitution of the Organization of American States is perhaps
sufficient commentary on the wisdom of our many military
interventions in the Caribbean, and President Wilson's
resort to the ABC (Argentina, Brazil and Chile) conference
in 1915—which rescued us from an ugly situation in Mexico
—sufficient commentary on the wisdom of the Pershing
expedition into Mexico. Once again we may ask, would we
do this now? The hapless Jacob Abrams was sentenced to
twenty years in jail (this was in 1919) for distributing leaf-
lets criticizing the Archangel and Siberian expeditions. At
the time he had only the consolation of being the occasion
for one of the greatest of all Justice Holmes's opinions. If
he were living now he might have the dubious consolation
of knowing that almost everyone agrees with his argument;
certainly we have paid a high price in the long-range en-
mity of the Soviet for that particular folly. Clearly a strong
case can be made out for Franklin D. Roosevelt's destroyer-
bases exchange and for extending protection to Greenland
and Iceland, but is it conceivable that the Congress would
have denied him the right to carry through these programs?

    If we turn to the many examples of presidential war-
making in the past twenty years we are impressed by the
fact that in almost every instance when the President put
his decision into effect, the Congress was actually in session
and available for consultation: thus the Korean intervention,
the landing of troops in Lebanon, the Bay of Pigs, the occu-

pation of the Dominican Republic by President Johnson, and the successive series of forays into Vietnam, Cambodia and Laos.

This view, to be sure, omits consideration of Lincoln's use of the executive power to meet the crisis of secession. Whether Lincoln was wise not to call the Congress into session for four months is still debated. Perhaps it can be said that the use of executive authority to put down a domestic insurrection rests on somewhat stronger constitutional arguments than those used to justify the use of force against China in 1900 or Vietnam in 1964.

There is one further observation that is relevant and may be instructive. Almost every instance of the use of presidential force in the past has been against small, backward, and distraught peoples—just the situation today. Call the role of the victims of presidential application of force in the past: Spanish Florida, Honduras, Santo Domingo, Nicaragua, Panama, Haiti, Guatemala, a China torn by civil war, a Mexico torn by civil war, a Russia and a Vietnam riven by civil war. It is a sobering fact that Presidents do not thus rush in with the weapons of war to bring Britain, France, Italy, modern Russia or Japan to heel. Would we have bombarded Southampton to collect a debt? Would we have sent an expedition into Rome to protect Americans against a threat from a Fascist government? Would we have precipitated a war with Britain over a boundary dispute in Maine? Would we land marines in France if customs collectors did not behave themselves? Would we bomb Siberia for years if shots were fired— without any hits—at an American vessel? And does it really comport with the honor and the dignity of a great nation to indulge its chief executive in one standard of conduct for the strong and another for the weak?

Clearly this record does not justify Mr. Katzenbach's rosy view of the use of presidential authority in the arena of foreign affairs, nor is there a single instance that bears out Senator McGee's assertion that "on more than one occasion the time allotted by crisis . . . has been less than the time it would take to assemble a quorum of the Congress."

Whether such a situation might arise in the future we do not have to determine. For Senator Javits' bill (S.731) makes ample provision for such an emergency by specifically authorizing the President to act "to repel a sudden attack against the United States" or "against the armed forces of the United States" when "*lawfully* stationed on foreign territory."

In his minority report on the Senate resolution limiting the power of the President to make national commitments on his own, Senator McGee speaks of S.85's "capabilities of mischief making." I have no doubt that the same argument will be brought against S.731. It is the argument almost invariably used against a proposal to limit the executive power. That S.85 and S.731 contain ambiguities cannot be denied. If we were to reject every constitutional provision, every guaranty of rights, every law that was ambiguous, we should have to settle for anarchy. Professor Thomas Reed Powell, of Harvard Law School, used to advise his students not to read the Constitution, as "it tends to confuse the mind." Indeed, it does. The senator does not, I presume, reject "commerce among the several states," "the general welfare," and "the establishment of religion" because the phrases forever elude final precision. Saint Matthew's reference to "blind guides who strain at a gnat and swallow a camel" is a fitting description of those who find quite acceptable the constitutional provision that "the executive power shall be vested in a President," but find the carefully drawn and precise language of S.85 and S.731 dangerously vague.

"Reason may mislead us. Experience must be our guide," said James Madison at the Constitutional Convention. By "reason" he meant theory or doctrine. Experience must indeed be our guide, and on the basis of a century and three-quarters of experience, confirmed by a quarter century of intensive modern experience, we can say with some confidence:

1. That with the exceptions of the Civil War—a special case—and perhaps of the Korean war—where the President responded to the decision of the Security Council—there are no instances in our history in which the use of war-making powers by the executive without authority of Congress was clearly and incontrovertibly required by the nature of the emergency which the nation faced. On the contrary, in almost every instance the long-term interests of the nation would have been better promoted by consultation and delay.

2. That great principles of government are not to be decided on the basis of the *argumentum ad horrendum*—by conjuring up hypothetical dangers and insisting that the structure and operation of government must be based on the chance of these rather than on experience. It was to this kind of argument that Thomas Jefferson said, "Shake not your raw-head and bloody-bones at me."

3. But that if such an emergency were to arise, it is amply provided for by the provisions of Senate Bill 731.

What Justice Jackson said in the steel-seizure case is relevant now as then: "We may say that power to legislate for emergencies belongs in the hands of Congress, but only Congress itself can prevent power from slipping through its fingers."

First, we should support Senate Bill 85—which the Senate adopted in June 1969 by an overwhelming majority, but which has so far been ineffective—and the proposed Senate Bill 731.

Second, let the Senate meet the argument of emergency, hypothetical as it is, by creating a permanent committee, a quorum of whose members would remain permanently in Washington, with authority to require that the President consult with the Senate or the Congress before taking any action that might involve the nation in armed conflict. Such a committee could be counted on to respond to a genuine emergency just as promptly as would the President, and counted on, too, to present the case for caution.

Third, let the Senate create a standing committee to consult with the President on all executive agreements, and with authority to designate those of sufficient importance to require submission to the Senate as treaties.

Fourth, the Congress must reinvigorate the power of the purse, that power which, as James Madison said, "may be regarded as the most complete and effectual weapon with which any constitution can arm the immediate representatives of the people," and that it use with more particularity than in the past the power to limit the place and the manner of the introduction and use of American arms and armed forces.

One final observation. The problems that confront us cannot be solved by debates over precedents, by appeals to constitutional probity, or by confronting presidential power with congressional: these may mitigate but will not resolve our crisis. All of these gestures address themselves to symptoms rather than to the fundamental disease. That disease is the psychology of the cold war; that disease is our obsession with power; that disease is our assumption that the great problems that glare upon us so hideously from every corner of the horizon can be solved by force.

The Defeat of America

American scholars are increasingly asking themselves the question that German scholars have been asking for the past quarter century: How explain the catastrophe? For while the American involvement in Southeast Asia is materially catastrophic, chiefly for Asians, morally it is a catastrophe for the American people analogous to that which so profoundly disturbed thoughtful and historical-minded Germans such as Meinecke or Gerhard Ritter or Theodor Litt.

A basic difference in the inquiry is that while the German conscience could not find expression until after the ultimate defeat—a form of catharsis not very helpful to the victims of the Nazi terror—the American conscience— thanks to the still surviving freedoms of inquiry and of criticism, thanks to *The New York Times*, thanks to such congressmen as Senator Gravel, and to such civil servants as Daniel Ellsberg, and to universities which still shelter dissident scholars—prospectively rather than retrospectively may

First printed in slightly different form in *New York Review of Books*, November 5, 1972.

be effective in mitigating the ravages of American policies. It is perhaps a measure of the iniquity of this war that the upsurge of conscience against it is more pervasive and more vigorous than in any previous wars, even misguided wars like those with Mexico, Spain and the Philippines. That is, however, small comfort to the victims of American terror.

No other war in which we have ever been engaged, except possibly the Civil War, poses so many or such difficult problems to the historian as does our ten-year war in Southeast Asia. With all the others the causes have seemed comprehensible, the conduct unexceptionable, the objectives plausible. The Vietnam war alone seems to be the product of willful folly, hysteria and paranoia, lacking in logic, purpose or objective, and waged with insensate fury against victims with whom we had no quarrel and who are incapable of doing us any physical or even any philosophical harm, waged for its own sake, or for the sake of "honor" which we have already forfeited or of "victory" forever elusive. What dramatizes and magnifies the demented quality of the war is that it was fought with mounting fury after whatever rationale it ever pretended to have—that of "containing" China—had been officially abandoned.

The psychological and moral questions which this war poses will probably never be fully answered. Why did the United States transfer the cold war from the Soviet Union to China? Events of 1972 demonstrate that there never was any logic—except domestic political logic—behind this; we could just as readily have accepted Communist China in 1952 as in 1972. Why did American statesmen ever suppose that we had either the right or the competence to be an Asian power? We would, after all, consider any Chinese statesman who thought that China should be an American power bereft of his senses. If we were prepared to fight an ideological war in Asia, why did we pick on Laos and Vietnam as our enemies instead of China itself? If our purpose is to establish an outpost of freedom and democracy in Asia, why do we support one of the most ruthless dictators and one of the most corrupt and reactionary regimes in Asia, and why, for that matter, did we rally to the support of a totalitarian Pakistan rather than a democratic India?

Why have we grown increasingly callous to crimes against humanity which we ourselves outlawed at Nuremberg and Tokyo, and why are we indifferent to the destruction of a small country onto which we poured the equivalent of two Hiroshima bomb loads every month? Why did we persist in a war which President Johnson by his cessation of bombing and President Nixon by his rapprochement with China acknowledged to be pointless? And how did it happen that after popular disillusionment with the war persuaded one President to retire and another to come into office with a promise to "end the war," we continued the war for four more years, in the process dropping more bombs on North and South Vietnam than ever before?

If the war violates the logic of politics and of morals, it violates just as flagrantly the logic of our history, and, if we may use the term, of our character. Perhaps, to be sure, we have deceived ourselves about that character all along; doubtless the American Indians would say this, and American blacks as well. But there is an almost perverse inconsistency in the spectacle of a people about to rededicate themselves with great fanfare to the "principles of seventy-six" devoting themselves so contumaciously to making shambles of those principles.

Traditionally the United States has been committed to the principle of negotiation rather than the resort to force in international disputes. We did, after all, arrange the first international negotiating commission at the time of the Jay Treaty, and we were chiefly instrumental in setting up the Hague Tribunal. But in our relations with Vietnam we have ignored the provisions of the United Nations Charter and a series of overtures from U Thant, refused to submit our dispute to outside arbitration and frustrated all meaningful negotiation by insisting that we negotiate on terms palpably unacceptable to North Vietnam because based on the premise that we have defeated it.

Traditionally we have avoided involvement in the internal affairs of Asia—a policy confirmed by the futility of our long championship of Chiang Kai-shek. Instead of taking heed of our own experience, and of the experience of the French in Vietnam, we permitted ourselves to be drawn into a conflict in many ways the most costly in our history, certainly the most frustrating, the most divisive, and morally the most indefensible.

We had ourselves been the first colony to throw off the yoke of colonialism, and we were the first nation to get rid of colonies altogether (we called them states instead), and outside our own hemisphere we boasted a long record of hostility to imperialism and colonialism—a hostility which Franklin Roosevelt concentrated heavily on European nations with colonies and empires in Asia. Yet we allowed ourselves to act first as surrogate for French colonialism in Vietnam, and then took over completely from the French. We tried to create all along the periphery of China a system of satellites, or puppet states, analogous to that of the puppet states which the Soviet maintains along her western borders —among them South Korea, the Philippines, Taiwan, Thailand, Laos, Cambodia, and South Vietnam. Will Mr. Nixon invite representatives from these states to participate in our bicentennial celebrations as the Russians invite representatives from their puppet states to participate in celebrations of the triumph of Communist ideology?

We had traditionally supported revolution—in Latin America, in France, Greece, Italy, Hungary, even in Ireland, though not in Russia—that was probably the turning point. Now we associate revolution with communism and oppose it, unless it is reactionary or military. Thus we supported Balaguer in Santo Domingo, Chiang Kai-shek in China, Franco in Spain, Salazar and Caetano in Portugal, Colonel Armas in Guatemala, the Colonels in Greece and the Generals in Brazil, and, of course, Thieu in Vietnam. The nation which fought the first revolution and which carried through a peaceful domestic revolution as well has become the leading opponent of revolution throughout the globe.

We had a record going back to the Civil War of trying to mitigate the ravages of war by the establishment of humane standards for civilians, and at Nuremberg we undertook to outlaw as crimes against humanity such acts as indiscriminate bombing of nonmilitary objectives, mistreatment of prisoners, and reprisals against whole communities for the alleged misdeeds of individuals. We are now bombing rural hamlets and villages indiscriminately (that is the meaning of a "free fire" zone), dropping napalm and "daisy-cutter" bombs whose only use is the killing or maiming of civilians, using defoliants and herbicides guaranteed to impair the ecology for a century and destroying Vietnam with an overkill prohibited by the laws of war which we ourselves prescribed. We had established the principle of accountability for "aggressive war" and for crimes against humanity at the German and Japanese war trials, convicted over 500,000 Nazis of crimes, hanged a score of them, and sentenced 720 Japanese officers to death. But so far the only war criminal to be brought to accountability in this war, for activities which cover the span of lawlessness from the destruction of villages to the massacre of civilians, is a lieutenant whose punishment is hardly that meted out to General Yamashita or to Karl Franck, hanged for the massacre at Lidice.

We had written into our Constitution the principle of the supremacy of the civilian over the military authority. The constitutional provision still stands, but has been in large part circumvented by the willing acquiescence of two successive Commanders in Chief in the exercise of independent authority by the Pentagon and the CIA in areas heretofore thought to be the domain of civil authority. Much of the emergence of military power has been the consequence of drift rather than of calculation. When Washington became President the United States Army consisted of fewer than 1,000 men and officers. Now ours is the largest and most powerful military establishment in the world. It absorbs one-third the budget, maintains its own foreign-affairs policy, and even instigates wars and supports revolutions without the knowledge of the Congress to whom is assigned the authority to declare war. There has been no formal repudiation of the principle of the supremacy of the civilian over the military, but we delude ourselves if we think the principle still means what the Founding Fathers supposed it to mean.

The generation that made the nation considered secrecy in government one of the instruments of Old World tyranny and committed itself to the principle that a democracy cannot function unless the people are permitted to know what their government is up to. Now almost everything that the Pentagon and the CIA do, and much that the President does, is shrouded in secrecy. Not only are the American people not permitted to know what they are up to but even the Congress and, one suspects, the President (witness the "unauthorized" bombing of the North in the fall and winter of '71) are kept in darkness.

Even more serious is the practice of evasion, distortion, and duplicity, which has become the almost official policy of the government from the White House down through the whole executive department and military establishment, a policy whose dimensions and character are documented in those Pentagon Papers whose full publication the government so desperately resisted. Certainly the most conspicuous feature of the Vietnam landscape today is not the millions of craters which make the land look like the surface of the moon but the fog of deception and lies that hangs over it. The Nixon administration did not formulate this violent departure from and repudiation of tradition. Still it has eagerly welcomed it—welcomed, that is, the rejection of the pragmatic approach to politics and the uncritical embrace of absolutes. When William James said, "Damn the Absolute," he spoke for most of his countrymen. Through most of our history the axiom "Theory may mislead us, experience must be our guide" has been controlling. The one major departure from it, the state sovereignty theories of the antebellum South, led to disaster. But much of the cold war, and the entire logic of the Vietnam war, is the product of abstractions and of absolutes, from the early theories about Chinese infiltration, or the domino theory, or the American commitment, to the theories of "Vietnamization," of "peace," and of "honor."

How are we to explain this almost convulsive break with what we considered to be our most familiar habits and our most deeply held convictions? Have the pressures of the cold war—a war which eventually encompassed most of the globe and thus for the first time gave us an opportunity to feel paranoid—worked fundamental changes in the American character in the past quarter century, or have those ingredients of interest and emotion and character which led us into the cold war in the first place and then persuaded us to plunge into the quagmire of the Vietnam war been latent in our character all along?

Mr. Barnet in his *The Roots of War* draws on both these explanations, but relies chiefly on the first. War, he submits, is a social institution and cannot be understood outside the social structure of which it is an integral part. This is a somewhat circular argument, but perhaps none the worse for that: a particular social culture nourishes war, and war in turn transforms the social culture. Certainly the American culture since 1940 is in considerable part a product of World War II and, even more, of the responsibilities and opportunities created by that war, of the unique position assigned by circumstances to the United States, of changes in technology and in the structural relations of the military with the economic interests that emerged out of the war. The postwar culture was, in turn, the setting of the cold war and of its almost Strangelovian by-product, the war in Vietnam.

It was increasingly not only a war economy that flourished after 1945 but a war psychology. War had taken command—the fear of war, the prospects of war, the requirements of war, the conduct of war, and, in the end, the ardor for war. We had always thought of ourselves as the most successful of nations; now war required that we be Number One in a very hard sense, not only as against any other nation but as against any combination of nations. Fear of war (which was quickly institutionalized into the cold war) required that we build up alliances everywhere—NATO, SEATO, CENTO, OAS (it was a kind of compulsive busyness)—and that we insist that neutrals be either with us or against us. War psychology in turn justified extending the subversive activities of the CIA into scores of countries. It required hundreds of bases around the globe—eventually some 400 major bases and almost 2,000 minor installations. With these we might have echoed Horace Walpole's boast after the peace of 1763, "Throw away your Greek and Roman books, histories of little peoples." War made insatiable demands on the economy, on the budget and on the intelligence establishment. War required ever tighter "security" measures, for who knew what enemies might be lurking at home? War pleaded the cause of military, not civilian, needs, and chose for the highest positions military, not civilian, leaders. The psychology of war even more than its material requirements shifted the center of gravity from the State

Department to the Pentagon, perhaps from the Congress to the Pentagon, possibly even from the White House to the Pentagon.

To take care of all of this there emerged a new security bureaucracy made up for the most part of the most distinguished men, recruited from the most distinguished universities, the most successful law firms, the richest banks, the most powerful corporations. They had too, for the most part, impeccable social credentials. If not all of them were Dean Achesons, that great gentleman was their ideal and their model, and every President except Franklin Roosevelt—who was an even greater swell than Acheson and who was not bemused by social pretensions—was duly impressed by him. For all their education and their sophistication, their high sense of personal integrity and personal honor, these security bureaucrats adopted uncritically the war psychology and lent their great talents not to devising ways of reducing tensions and avoiding war, but to ways of exacerbating tensions and preparing for war and—when it didn't come fast enough— making war. With so much going for war, it inevitably came, and thus the security managers were triumphantly vindicated in their apprehensions and their prophecies.

Those who prepared for war, and then embraced it, were not conscious war mongers; they were leaders of a bureaucracy which operated impersonally and almost mechanically, and which, in the end, had a life of its own. That is the way we have fought our ten-year war, impersonally and mechanically. For in this Alice-in-Wonderland bureaucratic world you achieve peace through war, order through chaos, security through violence, the reign of law through lawlessness; you preserve honor by dishonorable acts, and in the end you save Vietnam by destroying her.

Mr. Barnet's *Roots of War* is an enlarged, modernized version of the thesis which E. A. Ross propounded in his brilliant but neglected book *Sin and Society* back in 1907; that the most immoral acts are committed not by hardened criminals but by impeccable gentlemen who preside affably over great corporations, and who sin impersonally and at a great remove in time, in space—and in law—from the consequences of their crimes. Neither the iniquity nor the lawlessness of their conduct ever obtrudes upon them—the bribing of fire inspectors, or the selling of adulterated goods or habit-forming drugs, sending children down into the mine shafts, condemning girls to work twelve hours a day in sweatshops, bribing policemen, corrupting legislators, profiting from war.

"Those responsible for these crimes never think of themselves as criminals," Ross said, "nor are they ever punished, even by public disapproval. On the contrary they sit on the boards of foundation and accept honorary degrees from universities, they are welcomed into the best clubs and the most fashionable churches," "Those who plan do not kill," writes Mr. Barnet, "and those who kill do not plan," so all can have peace of mind. There was something of this in Hiroshima and Nagasaki, to be sure, but never before in history has a nation been systematically destroyed as Vietnam was destroyed, by high-minded gentlemen animated more by sorrow than by anger as they directed their computerized technology to deliver their surgical strikes. "Upon their gentlemanly presence," as Ross wrote, "the eventual blood and tears do not obtrude themselves."

And if the ultimate verdict on the security bureaucracy is that they debased the moral standards and tarnished the honor of their country by their crimes, the immediate verdict must surely be that they did not even achieve the ends they sought. As Barnet writes:

The generation in which the United States spent 1,500 billion dollars on armaments witnessed a sharp increase in threats to national security, an erosion of United States military and political power, and serious cracks in the United States corporate economy itself. The very longevity of the national security managers has helped to compound and finally to enshrine their failures. There was no room in the official orthodoxy even to contemplate the changes in the political organization of the planet that are needed for survival, and no interest in trying to bring them about.

On all this what Woodrow Wilson said to Frank Cobb on the eve of the First World War is still valid: "What does it mean to go to war? It means an attempt to reconstruct a peacetime civilization with war standards, and at the end of the war there will be no bystanders with sufficient peace standards left to work with. There will be only war standards."

The second major interest which nourishes the roots of war, and war itself, is economic—a new version, this, of that nineteenth-century cliché, economic imperialism. Classical mercantilism had dictated expansion and empire and war where that was necessary for reasons of state. Originally such mercantilists as Colbert, Frederick the Great, or Hamilton regarded the profit of trading companies or of individuals as incidental to the national purpose. Now mercantilism has come full circle. Where business expansion, colonies, alliances were designed to strengthen the state, now the state is required to build armaments, maintain enormous armies, make alliances, subvert governments, launch overseas ventures, be prepared for wars and on occasion fight them in order to sustain the economy and to support those great corporate enterprises that dominate the economy.

It is a familiar story, this partnership of government and business in the conduct of foreign policy. But certainly the alliance is more intimate now than it was in the days when Henry Demarest Lloyd wrote *Wealth Against Common-*

wealth and David Graham Phillips published his exposé *The Treason of the Senate* and William Jennings Bryan thundered vainly against Wall Street—more intimate because more pervasive, more sophisticated, and more profitable.

The military-industrial complex of Eisenhower's last public speech has become a military-industrial-labor complex. It has enlisted not only such likely senators as Henry Jackson but less likely ones such as Hubert Humphrey; it has even enlisted George Meany himself, whose zeal for the war may not be wholly disinterested. More, and more somberly, it has made an alliance with universities and research institutes, which are thus more and more dependent on the military for financing, and whose ultimate by-products may be beneficial to man but whose immediate products often are not. Perhaps the greatest tribute to the astuteness of American capitalism—an astuteness far less overwhelming in the economic than in the political arena—is that it has learned how to make everybody profit from war except its victims and later generations.

But do Americans really profit from war and preparation for war? Surely profit is an illusion here, as victory in war is an illusion. For the cost of war and of preparation for war is far higher than the 15 hundred billion dollars which we have spent in the last thirty years. It includes the tangible burdens, such as payment on the debt, which is saddled on fuutre generations—Nixon's business-minded administration managed to add almost 100 billions to that debt in four years —or the increased cost of everything, or the ceaseless waste of the natural resources of the entire globe. It includes impalpable but ultimately more costly things, such as the waste of talent and of labor on the 'work of destruction rather than their application to the work of construction; the distraction of the best minds of this and other nations from the tasks of true statesmanship; and the steady deterioration in the quality of life for the majority of the American people, not to mention the Vietnamese. It includes forcing other nations to follow the American example of distraction and waste in sheer self-defense; just think what the American strategy in the Far East has cost China in the past twenty years. Mr. Barnet relegates this point, oddly enough, to a footnote: "The most crucial intellectual and political task of the 1970's is the development of an alternative vision of a world economy based on the values of just distribution of economic and political power, and the priority of human growth over economic growth."

In that distant past before World War II an open alliance between the White House, the regulatory commissions, government bureaucracy, corporate capitalism, and the press would have been politically dangerous, if not fatal. Now such a network of alliances is regarded as inevitable and, on the whole, benevolent. How has it happened that this generation of Americans is prepared to accept what earlier generations found reprehensible?

The story of the manipulation of public opinion is a chilling one, for it makes clear that even in a country where all channels of communication are technically open, and where the press is as "free" as it is anywhere else in the world, and where the Academy and the scientific community are strong and independent, government is still able to influence the flow of news, to withhold or distort facts and to manipulate public opinion.

The philosophy of the information managers is much the same as the philosophy of the war managers; they are parts of the same bureaucratic machine and almost interchangeable parts. And just as the war was never presented to the American people as a real war but as a crusade, or a rescue operation for the embattled South Vietnamese, or resistance to aggression, or honoring a commitment, or, perhaps, as a useful exercise in technological warfare, so the information bureaucracy does not concern itself with the real United States, the real government, the real economy, the real inflation or the real crime rate, but always with an image of these things, concocted by Madison Avenue experts and as phony as their advertising claims.

Under the Nixon administration government itself has come to be increasingly a public relations job, with great issues of foreign and domestic policy packaged and sold by fanfare and catchwords much as cereals and detergents are sold. No administration in our history has so blatantly revealed its contempt for the intelligence of the American people as this one has by its manipulation of the news, its corruption of the language and its unabashed propaganda.

No wonder the information bureaucracy hates a free press or an uncontrolled television, for these threaten the packaged image which the information experts have concocted by presenting, instead, the real thing. Happily— from their point of view—they have vast resources with which to defend themselves, and the people, against the perils of truth.

Never before in our own history has government employed so many methods for manipulating and distorting the truth as during the past decade, not even during the First and Second World Wars. The position of the past two administrations is well expressed by General Maxwell Taylor: "A citizen should know those things he needs to know to be a good citizen and to discharge his functions." Who decides what he needs to know and how he is to discharge his functions, General Taylor did not say. It is not, indeed, clear what such assorted news managers as Nixon, Mitchell, Kleindienst, Laird, and others of their ilk think the citizen needs to know, but it is clear by now what they think he does not need to know: what is in the Pentagon Papers, and all the papers related to the conduct of war and of foreign policy.

How does government go about its work of evasion, suppression, deception and manipulation of news? It is of course immensely powerful and rich, and it can hire all the news managers it needs. The President himself can always command the media and can always be sure that whatever he says will be heard or read in millions of homes and accorded the respect that ordinarily attaches to presidential statements rather than that which it deserves. For notwithstanding the long record of duplicity, so strong is the traditional confidence in the President that even Johnson and Nixon are given the benefit of the doubt. The information bureaucracy commands almost limitless funds; the Pentagon alone spends some four billion dollars a year on news, propaganda, and, doubtless, secrecy.

Secrecy is, clearly, the easiest way to manage the news and to make sure that public opinion does not go astray, and secrecy is now fundamental not only to the conduct of the war but to the conduct of foreign and even of domestic affairs. Secrecy—as the Pentagon Papers make clear—has presided over almost the whole of our intervention in Southeast Asia from the fifties on: over the prolonged war in Laos, over the nature of our support to the French, over our support to—and abandonment of—the miserable Diem, over the Tonkin Bay caper—a put-up job if there ever was one—over our invasion of Cambodia and the rationale for it, over the peace overtures and negotiations, and over their breakdown too. Nor is secrecy confined to the war in Vietnam. It beclouds our commitments to Greece, Spain and Brazil, and conceals from all but the most pertinacious the long-range plans for the training of mercenary armies in Southeast Asia or for our own weaponry.

Along with secrecy goes deceit. No other administration in our history has practiced deception, duplicity, chicanery and mendacity as has the Nixon administration. Where totalitarian regimes invented the technique of the Big Lie, this administration has developed a more effective technique, that of lies so innumerable that no one can keep up with them, so insolent that they confound refutation, and so shameless that in time they benumb the moral sensibilities of the American people.

Corruption reveals itself first in language. Thucydides so said in that memorable paragraph on the extravagances of revolutionary zeal: "What used to be described as a thoughtless act of aggression was now regarded as the courage one would expect to find in a party member; to think of the future . . . was merely one way of saying one was a coward. Fanatical enthusiasm was the mark of a real man . . . anyone who held violent opinions could always be trusted and . . . to plot successfully was a sign of intelligence."

Corruption of language is a special form of deception which this administration, through its Madison Avenue mercenaries, has brought to a high point of perfection. Bombing is "protective reaction," precision bombing is "surgical strikes," concentration camps are "pacification centers" or "refugee camps," just like our "relocation" camps for the Nisei in World War II. Bombs dropped outside the target area are "incontinent ordnance," and those dropped on a South Vietnam village are excused as "friendly fire"; a bombed house becomes automatically a "military structure" and a lowly sampan sunk on the waterfront a "waterborne logistic craft." How sobering that fifteen years before 1984 our own government should invent a doublethink as dishonest as that imagined by Orwell.

Even more dangerous than secrecy and deception (happily there will always be Ellsbergs and Jack Andersons to uncover them) is the deliberate effort of the administration to intimidate the press and the television networks—intimidation by the McCarthy-like slurs and innuendos of an Agnew, intimidation by suits against *The New York Times* and Daniel Ellsberg for their part in making the Pentagon Papers available to the public (how illuminating that in the

Ellsberg trial the government wanted to eliminate jurors who had read *The New York Times*!), intimidation by the misuse of grand juries to go on hunting expeditions against all who have been involved in crusades against the Vietnam war or who were involved in the exploitation of the Pentagon Papers, as in the case of Senator Gravel. There is a special irony in such suits, for they are, of course, financed by the public, who are thus permitted to pay for the privilege of being kept in the dark about their own government. Never before in our history, it is safe to say, has government so contemptuously violated the spirit of the constitutional guarantee of freedom of the press.

For all this we are paying a high price on the domestic scene: loss of faith in the integrity of our government; loss of confidence in the ability of the press and television to retain their independence; erosion of the guarantees of the Bill of Rights and of the habit of taking those rights for granted; and worst of all, perhaps, denial of that access to information which the Founding Fathers rightly deemed essential to the operations of a democratic society. And on the international scene, too, secrecy and duplicity lead to a loss of confidence in the United States by other peoples and governments. What confidence can foreign chancelleries put in our declarations of policy after the revelations of duplicity in the India-Pakistan war, when we pretended to observe neutrality, but in fact "tilted toward Pakistan"—that is, toward the totalitarian, not the democratic, nation.

President Nixon never tires of ringing the changes on the tired argument that if we fail to live up to our "commitments" to South Vietnam we will forfeit the confidence of other nations who rely on us. We do not in fact have "commitments" that require us to intervene in the affairs of Vietnam. If we do, so have Britain and France, for both are signatories of the SEATO treaty, but neither reads that agreement as requiring military intervention. What do they make of an argument of "honor" which is itself rooted in deception?

Most of this, Mr. Barnet argues, is a product of the generation after Pearl Harbor, a generation that saw profound changes in the structure of the American government and economy and, by implication, in the American character itself. The argument is plausible and the evidence persuasive, for if wars do not themselves dramatically change the character of a society they do accelerate changes that are in the making; that seems to have been true from the Peloponnesian War to the American Civil War. And yet if we ask of this tragic chapter of our history through which we are now passing not so much what happened as why things happened the way they did, we shall have to look deeper into the American past than Mr. Barnet is willing to do. For if the immediate explanation of the Vietnam involvement is to be found in the structural changes of government and economy, and in the follies, vanities, errors, and presumptions of the new ruling elite, the roots go down into the deep subsoil of American history and culture.

It seems like a far cry from Jefferson and Tom Paine to L. B. Johnson and Richard Nixon, and indeed it is. But it is to Jefferson and Paine—as spokesmen and as symbols—that we turn for a formulation of those myths which, in vulgarized and perverted form, have presided over our misuse of power. The relevant myths—there are of course others—are the myth of innocence, the myth of destiny and the myth of moral superiority.

The myth of New World innocence and Old World depravity was born out of the struggle for independence and for nationalism, and runs like a golden thread through much of our history and our literature, with the gold getting more and more tarnished. What is taught is that Americans were chosen by Providence to conduct a great experiment designed to show what man might be if free from the tyrannies of the past—that is, of the Old World: despotism and class and war, poverty and ignorance and superstition. Carried to its logical extreme, it appeared to free America from the tyranny of history as well. "We have it in our power to begin the world anew," wrote Tom Paine exultantly. "A new era for politics is struck, a new method of thinking hath arisen." So too said Jefferson:

> If all the sovereigns of Europe were to set themselves to work to emancipate the minds of their subjects from their present ignorance and prejudices . . . a thousand years would not place them in that high ground on which our common people are now setting out.

This implied that we were no longer subject to the laws or the lessons of the past; that we could bestride History like a colossus or direct its current our way. It was Jefferson who elaborated this philosophy most consciously: because we were a chosen people, it was up to us to show what man was capable of when truly free, up to us to raise the standards to which all peoples and nations might ultimately aspire. Thus the sense (or the myth) of mission was inextricably fused with the sense of innocence. But how different the sense of mission and of destiny in Jefferson was from that which we find in our current leaders. Never for a moment did Jefferson allow his pride in America to betray him into the demented notion that Providence had somehow made it our responsibility to impose the American pattern of life on less fortunate peoples.

No, to Jefferson and his generation American power should reveal itself in the moral sphere, not in the political or the military. Our duty was not to impose our way of life on others but to present to the world the spectacle of peace and prosperity, freedom and justice, virtue and happiness, confident that eventually other nations would rally to the American standard. This was the theme of the last letter Jefferson wrote, just a few days before his death on July 4, 1826: America "will be to the world a signal for arousing men to burst the chains under which monkish ignorance and superstition had persuaded them to bind themselves, and to assume the blessings and security of self-government." Not material power but moral power was to spread American influence about the globe.

The myths of innocence and of destiny implied the myth of superiority, which has, however, its special, moving and tragic history. The notion itself can be traced to the "sifted grain" theory of the Puritans; it was strengthened by the teachings of the Enlightenment and by independence; and it was ratified by the incontestable success of the American experiment throughout most of the nineteenth century. After all, to most Americans, twenty-five million immigrants were a pretty convincing demonstration. Already they assumed that their government was more just, their society more enlightened, their morals more elevated than any others. All of this conveniently ignored slavery, and Americans early learned what they have now developed almost to a science —to ignore what might disturb the symmetry of their arguments or ruffle the surface of their self-esteem. Thus Mr. Nixon never ceases to assure us that "we are a peace-loving people."

Consciousness of moral superiority led inevitably to a double standard, for if our hearts were pure, our motives disinterested, and our purposes noble, what we did (however it might look to the uninitiated observer) could not be judged by the standards that history applied to the misdeeds of the corrupt nations of the Old World or, now, of Asia.

As William Vaughn Moody put it in his desperate protest against that Philippine war which was a kind of dry run for the Vietnam war:

Lies, lies, it cannot be! The wars we wage
Are noble, and our battles still are won
By justice for us . . .
We have not sold our loftiest heritage.
The proud republic hath not stooped to cheat
And scramble in the market-place of war,
Her forehead weareth yet its solemn star.

(Ode in Time of Hesitation)

Just what Mr. Nixon says every day—but, unlike Moody, he has conned himself into believing it, and what is worse, he has conned most of the American people into believing it, and into accepting unquestioningly the double standard. When the Soviet Union intervenes in Czechoslovakia, that is naked aggression, but when we land 22,000 marines in Santo Domingo, that is peace-keeping. When Communist countries carry on clandestine activities abroad, that is part of an "international conspiracy," but when the CIA operates clandestinely in sixty foreign countries, that is a legitimate function of our foreign policy. When Russia establishes a missile base in Cuba (on the invitaton of Cuba), that is an act of war which must be met with all the force at our command, but when we build the largest air base in the world in Thailand, that is part of our ceaseless search for peace. When China equips the armies of North Vietnam, that is a dangerous intervention in a foreign war, but when we provide South Vietnam with the largest active air force, the largest active fleet, the best equipment and weaponry in the world, and half a million soldiers besides, that is living up to our commitments. When North Vietnam refuses to surrender her POWs—something *we* have never done during a war—that is a sign of barbarism, but when we stand by while our puppet armies torture and cage and kill prisoners, that is a nice refusal to interfere in the conduct of a sovereign state.

When Germans wiped out defenseless villages as a reprisal for sniping or committed savage massacres, we condemned these as war crimes and punished them with death, but when we wipe out defenseless villages with "incontinent ordnance," or engage in massacres as brutal as that at Lidice, these are mistakes or aberrations that do not mar the record of our benevolence. When, in the spring of 1972, North Vietnam launched an invasion of the South, that was "aggression" of the most reckless character, but our bombings deep into North Vietnam, which had been going on for months in clear violation of whatever "understandings" we had arrived at, were merely "protective reaction." And so on *ad infinitum*.

President Nixon, like his predecessor, was determined that he should not go down in history as the man who presided over the first American "defeat." It is, alas, too late for such arguments, for nothing can alter the fact that we have already been defeated, not, to be sure, on the field of battle, but in the eyes of history. We did of course destroy much of Vietnam, but to call such insensate destruction victory is to fall back on the logic of Humpty Dumpty: "When I use a word it means just what I choose it to mean." And when, after ten years of meaningless and futile war we signed a "cease-fire" agreement, Mr. Nixon announced that we had won "Peace with honor."

But our concept of "honor," like our concept of "peace," is all part of a pattern of synthetic politics and synthetic morals appropriate to a war fought with impersonal technology over issues that no one can explain, supported by arguments that are spurious and by rhetoric that is canting and unctuous. Indeed, nothing about the conduct of the war is genuine or honest or real except the death and devastation we have poured into Vietnam: that is real.

This is not only a war we cannot win, it is a war we must lose if we are to survive morally. Ame:icans are of course spoiled by the habit of victory, and they have come to think of victory in war as guaranteed by the laws that regulate the cosmic system. An odd conviction, this, especially in such men as Dean Rusk or General Westmoreland or Strom Thurmond or Governor Wallace, for they cannot be unfamiliar with what is still called the "Lost Cause," or unaware that even the most fanatical Confederate flag-waving Dixiecrat would not really have it otherwise.

We honor now those Southerners who stood by the Union when it was attacked by the Confederacy, just as we honor those Germans who rejected Hitler and his monstrous wars and were martyrs to the cause of freedom and humanity. Why do we find it so hard to accept this elementary lesson of history, that some wars are so deeply immoral that they must be lost, that the war in Vietnam is one of these wars, and that those who resist it are the truest patriots? And of those who resist—often at the cost of their lives and their fortunes but not of their honor—may we not say what Pericles said in that noblest of all speeches, that they are fortunate in "knowing that the secret of happiness is freedom and the secret of freedom a brave heart, and they do not idly stand aside from the enemy's onset"?

The Shame
of the Republic

_____

Watergate, and all those attendant usurpations, sub-
versions and corruptions for which the word has become
both a symbol and a short cut, is neither a "deplorable incident"—to use Mr. Nixon's revealing phrase—nor an historical sport. It is a major crisis, constitutional, political and
moral—one that challenges our governmental system. Public
attention is, and will long remain, focused on what happened, but already the interest of publicists and scholars is
shifting to the more troublesome question of why it happened.

The roots of our current malaise go back to the paranoia
about communism—first Soviet, then Chinese—that obsessed
Americans after 1947. So deep and pervasive was this paranoia that—like the Southern commitment to slavery before
the Civil War and to white supremacy after the war—in
time it came to dominate our lives and our thoughts, and to
color our views of politics, economy, education, science and
morality. As in the worlds of Kafka and Orwell, it justified

First printed in slightly different form in _New York Review of Books_,
July 19, 1973.

adopting the tactics of the enemy in order to defeat him—
just what the Nixon administration has been doing for the
past four years, just what that half-baked "Jeffersonian lib-
eral" Mr. Thomas Huston achieved when he sold Mr. Nixon
a vast scheme of repression in order to avert repression. In
both the McCarthy and Watergate eras it has justified
undermining the Constitution and the Bill of Rights in order,
presumably, to save them.

Inevitably Watergate (perhaps we should find a different
name, like Nixonism) conjures up and reflects McCarthyism.
But something new has been added; indeed much has been
added that makes it more dangerous, more corrupt, and
more subversive than that earlier foray against sanity and
decency. For war has been added—a ten-year war which
benumbed the American conscience and blunted the American political intelligence.

The cold war itself was largely a product of deductive
and *a priori* reasoning, and therefore a self-delusion, and so
too, in added measure, was the ten-year war against Vietnam.
The doctrinaire state of mind lends itself eagerly to paranoia, for real dangers are nothing compared to those our
imagination can conjure up. It was almost inevitable that
the psychology which imagined the domino theory and en-
visioned a million Chinese landing (after a good healthy
swim) on the shores of California should see in every student demonstration, every sit-down at an airport or a napalm
factory, every exposure of government chicanery or of over-
runs in naval contracts, a threat to the survival of the republic. For if the threat of communism is so importunate
as to justify the longest war in which we have ever been
engaged, the satanic arsenal of weapons used against friends
and enemies indiscriminately, the use of napalm, the My
Lai and other massacres, the violations of international law
and of the laws of war, the destruction of a whole nation,
then surely it justifies such minor peccadilloes as wiretap-

ping, or the use of provocative agents, or breaking into safes, or the corruption of elections, or Watergate.

Basic to an understanding of the usurpations, duplicities, and irresponsibilities of the Nixon era, then, is paranoia, which has a life of its own, and which still lingers on—even after the "end" of the war and the rapprochement with China—polluting the moral and intellectual atmosphere of the country. Certainly there is little evidence that Mr. Nixon or his underlings think the new relationship with the Soviet Union and China justifies the mitigation of their own paranoia about "national security," or their conviction that any attack upon official policy is itself a potential threat to security. How else explain the vindictiveness of the prosecution of Daniel Ellsberg and the readiness to subvert justice in that prosecution; how else explain the political skulduggery that persisted long after the 1972 election, the persistent use of the FBI and the CIA for political purposes, the readiness to employ provocative agents, the contumacious boast at the POW dinner that reliance on secrecy, even useless secrecy, would go on and on; how else explain the determination to bomb Cambodia back to the Stone Age?

Successive Presidents have tried to wash their hands of personal responsibility for the lawlessness and corruption so pervasive in our government in the last decade or so. But whoever planned and launched the Bay of Pigs, whoever engineered the Tonkin Bay fraud, deceived the nation about the danger of communism in Santo Domingo, directed the secret war in Laos and fought a secret war in Cambodia, authorized the use of napalm and of free-fire zones, acquiesced in the torture and murder of prisoners; whoever concocted Watergate, rifled the safes, installed the bugging devices, planted the agents, accepted and paid bribes, doctored the polls and the cables—for all these, ultimate responsibility lodges in the White House. It is the President who sets the moral tone, who selects the assistants he wishes to work with him—above all the Attorneys General—and it is the President who profits from such successes as the chicaneries of his associates and subordinates may produce. It is the President, therefore who must be assigned responsibility not only for failures—as with the Bay of Pigs—or for violations of international law—as with Santo Domingo—but for debasing the political standards and polluting the moral atmosphere of the nation.

But it is insufficient to assign responsibility for our current sickness to particular Presidents. After all, it is the American people who elected them—in the case of Mr. Nixon, by the largest majority in our history. Two competing explanations, or at least illuminations, require consideration. One is that we are confronted not merely with personal offenses and particular failures but with a major breakdown in our constitutional and political mechanisms. The second is that our government and politics, with all their knaveries, vulgarities, and dishonesties, more or less reflect American society, and even the American character, and that we are, in fact, getting the kind of government that we want or deserve. The fault, in short, is in ourselves.

The first of these explanations lends itself more readily to analysis than the second. Put most simply it argues that a Constitution designed for the modest needs of a society of four million people, whose business was mostly farming, and whose political needs were adequately served by local and state governments, and based on the principle that government, like dress, was the badge of lost innocence, is no longer adequate to the importunate needs of a nation of 200 million for the operation of traditional democracy, or for the requirements of world power and of modern war. Thus those famous constitutional principles established in England and America in the seventeenth and eighteenth centuries—separation and balance of powers, limitations on government inscribed in bills of rights, restrictions on executive authority, especially in the realm of making war, legislative control of the purse, due process of law and the impartial rule of law—are dangerously out of date!

Equally out of date, so President Nixon proclaims by his conduct if not by his words, are those assumptions about the relations of men to government so fundamental that they were either taken for granted or left to the rhetoric of preambles and bills of rights rather than put into the body of the Constitution. Thus, with respect to the assumption that public servants are precisely that, the Virginia Bill of Rights puts it, "that all power is vested in and derived from the people; that magistrates are their trustees and servants, and at all times amenable to them." "Amenable" is not the word that pops into our minds when we contemplate Mr. Nixon, nor does he think of himself and of the Praetorian Guard with which he surrounds himself as servants. He regards the American people as essentially children; he treats their elected representatives with contempt; he says, in effect, that the people have no inherent right of privacy, no inherent right to differ or dissent on great issues of policy, no inherent right even to a free, open and honest ballot.

No less important, in the eyes of the Founding Fathers, was the assumption of candor and openness in government —the assumption, that is, that the people have a right to know. This was the reason for those provisions in almost every state constitution and in the Bill of Rights for freedom of the press; this was the logic behind Jefferson's famous statement that given a choice between a government without newspapers and newspapers without a government, he would choose the latter; this was the philosophy that animated that passion for education expressed by most of the constitution Makers: that without enlightenment about government, democracy simply would not work.

It is sometimes argued that the Constitution itself was drawn up in secret session. So it was. It was also debated in twelve state conventions during a period of a year, and by almost everyone who had participated in its making. Not only in the *Federalist Papers* but in scores of books and pamphlets every line and word of the document was subjected to the most searching scrutiny. No other political document of our history was more thoroughly—or more publicly—analyzed and explored. And, on the whole, since Washington, Presidents have faithfully continued this early tradition, though there are exceptions. The oft-cited case of Washington's "refusal" to make available to the Congress the papers bearing on the Jay Treaty is of course not an exception. Washington gave the Senate everything it asked for, and the House everything that bore on its constitutional authority to make appropriations. Just as Nixon's is the first administration in our history to attempt prior censorship of the press—*The New York Times* and *Washington Post*— and the first systematically to withhold from the Congress information it requires to fulfill its constitutional obligations, so it is the first to adopt wiretapping as an almost official political instrument, and to condone the habitual politics of lying.

All of this—so runs the argument—is rooted nevertheless not in the inadequacy or corruption of the men who happen to be in office at any moment but in the inadequacy and obsolescence of the anachronistic mechanisms with which we are saddled when we undertake to deal with the complex problems of modern economy, technology and war.

This brings us back to the central question: can we run a Leviathan state with an eighteenth-century Constitution?

Perhaps the obvious answer is also the right one: so far we have. Needless to say the Constitution is not merely the original document of 1787; it is also the score and more of amendments, some of them fundamental. It is the gloss of four hundred volumes of Supreme Court opinions. It is that organic growth presided over by President and Congress and not unacceptable to the Court. That growth has been extensive, even prodigious. In the case of the Civil War amendments, it has been revolutionary. But both the organic growth and the revolutions were constitutional. So too with such political revolutions as produced, over the years, judicial review, the transformation of the federal system and the evolution of the welfare state.

Is the crisis of the present so imperative that it requires an unconstitutional revolution—requires, that is, abandoning the separation of powers, discarding limitations on the executive authority, weakening legislative control of the purse, repealing the Bill of Rights, subverting the traditional rule of law, and covering with a fog of secrecy the operations of government? Clearly Mr. Nixon and a good many of his followers think that it is. Now we are back with the phobia about communism and paranoia about national security.

Each generation tends to think that the crisis which it happens to confront is the gravest in history, and ours is no exception. But nothing that we face today compares in gravity with the crisis of the Civil War—when it seemed that the nation might be rent asunder and slavery prosper—or the crises of the great depressions of the 1890s and the 1930s. All three of these were attended by political and constitutional revolution—the Civil War crisis by a very disorderly revolution, but constitutional nevertheless. It might well be questioned whether we even face a crisis today other than the crises we have masochistically brought upon ourselves—the crisis of the cold war, the crisis of our paranoia about China, the crisis of the reckless betrayal of our fiduciary obligation to posterity through the destruction of natural resources, the crisis of confidence in republican government brought about by unconstitutional war and unconstitutional domestic policies, the crisis of morals which is a product of all of these. It is of course all familiar enough: you create a real crisis by moving convulsively against an imaginary one.

There is no reason to suppose that the problems which confront us cannot be solved by regular political and constitutional means. While it is no doubt true that this administration would be unable to function as it has functioned over the past four years if it were required to observe the strict limits of the Constitution, the conclusion is not that we should therefore acquiesce in the relaxation of constitutional limits but that the administration should abide by them. For in every instance of administrative challenge to the Constitution and the Bill of Rights it was the challenge that proved disastrous, not the limitation.

Would we be worse off if Nixon had confined himself to the constitutional limitations of his office? Would we be worse off if he had been unable to wage war in Laos, invade and bomb Cambodia, mine Haiphong Harbor; spread a pall of secrecy over not only military but domestic operations that had any connection with "national security"; establish censorship in many areas of governmental operations; use the CIA not only to subvert foreign governments but in domestic politics, and violate the constitutional obligation to "make a regular Statement of all . . . Expenditures of all public Money" with respect to the five or six billion dollars which the CIA annually spends; destroy domestic programs that the Congress had voted by impounding appropriations; authorize wiretaps on foreign embassies, congressmen, the National Security Council, newsmen, and others; invoke executive privilege, and spread the mantle of executive immunity over his henchmen; use *agents provocateurs* to smoke out "antiwar radicals," and subvert the processes of justice by turning the Justice Department into a political agency?

What Mr. Nixon complains of being unable to do under a strict interpretation of the Constitution is precisely what those who wrote the Constitution intended he should be unable to do.

Yet we cannot ignore the fact that one part of the Constitution has always given us trouble, and that is precisely the provision for the executive and for executive power. In no other area has the Constitution had to be so patched up—four amendments, no less, all dealing with the executive branch—this compared to one dealing with the judiciary (and that speedily nullified) and one—popular election of senators—dealing with the legislative. Not surprising; after all, the office was new, and with the possible exception of some American states, unprecedented; after all, everyone took for granted that Washington would be the first President, and there he sat, presiding over the Convention, the very symbol of rectitude; after all, there were as yet no national parties to take charge of elections and even of administrations.

The framers were confronted by an almost insoluble dilemma: fear that power always corrupts and awareness that the man who presided over their deliberations and would be the first President was incorruptible; conviction that the executive power, especially in the area of making war, was highly dangerous, and awareness that Washington had already demonstrated that with a man of honor there was no danger. Nor could they devise any method which would ensure that they would always have a Washington—or an Adams, a Jefferson, a Madison—in the presidential chair.

They took refuge, therefore, in studied ambiguity, and ambiguity has presided over the executive power from that day to this. Consider, for example, the problem of the executive power in foreign relations. It is, said Woodrow Wilson a century or so later, "very absolute"; clearly Mr. Nixon thinks so too. But it rests on very uncertain constitutional authority, for that document says merely that the President shall be Commander in Chief (which does not necessarily concern the conduct of foreign relations), that he shall, with the advice and consent of the Senate, appoint ambassadors and make treaties, and that he shall receive ambassadors. That is the whole of it—and what a superstructure has been reared on that foundation!

The dilemma persists. To allow the President to take us into war, as he did on two recent occasions, is to invite disaster; to tie his hands in emergencies is also to invite disaster. Experience, to be sure, has so far exemplified only the first, not the second, of these dangers. Perhaps such a bill as the Javits-Stennis War Powers Act may at least mitigate the problem, but it is improbable that any legislation can deal adequately with the many-sided façade of executive powers as well as with complex problems of tenure, removal, impeachment, succession, and so forth. Perhaps in this respect the only ultimate reassurance can come in a courageous and revitalized Congress, a truly independent judiciary, and that eternal vigilance which the Founding Fathers took for granted.

Watergate, then, cannot be explained merely as the consequence of incompetence or knavery of men in high office; these terms can be applied to the Grant and Harding administrations as well, when not only the republic but the presidency survived and flourished. Nor can the American people so easily shift responsibility onto Mr. Nixon. After all he had not led a precisely private life, and 42 million Americans who should or could have been familiar with his public career after 1946 voted for him. Surely we must assume that they knew what they were about and that they got what they wanted.

Nor can Watergate be explained as the result of intolerable stresses and strains on our constitutional and political mechanisms; these have held up under far greater strains during the Depression and the Great War, and indeed it is not the Constitution and laws that have failed us, but persistent resort to lawlessness.

A third possible explanation is that responsibility for our crisis is rooted in changes in the American character, the American mind, American habits or traits—use what term you will—over the past quarter century, that are reflected in Mr. Nixon and his associates and in the current style of American politics.

Much here is in the realm of conjecture, for to fix national traits is like fixing quicksilver, and to go on from there to trace cause and effect is almost to indulge in mysticism. Yet, at some moments of history anyway, national styles do seem to be reflected in politics: the style of the Old South, for example, in the politics of slavery; the style of Bismarck's Germany in the war and diplomacy of the last half of the nineteenth century—how different from the almost music-box Germany of early romanticism; the style of the Japan that launched the great Pacific war. Styles change, and have in the South, in Germany, and in Japan. If Jefferson is a representative figure of the American Enlightenment, faithfully reflecting its virtues, its optimisms, its faiths, its limitations, so perhaps Mr. Nixon is a representative figure of contemporary America, reflecting its arrogance, its violence, its passion for manipulation, its commercialism, but not reflecting its generosity or idealism or intellectual ferment.

Consider first something very large, the shift in the concept of America's role in history, and of the American "mission." To Jefferson's generation that role was clear—to provide a moral example to the peoples of the world. The American empire was, in the almost hackneyed phrase of the Founding Fathers, an Empire of Reason. Mr. Nixon too believes in an American mission. That mission is to be achieved, however, not by reason but by power—force at home to whip recalcitrants into line, force abroad to whip lesser breeds into line—force in such little things as breaking into safes, force in such big things as building the greatest arsenal in the history of the world.

The corruption of the Jeffersonian view of mission emerges wherever we look: for moral mission, the military; for a unique vision of self-government, hostility throughout the globe to the forces of popular insurgency; for a welcome to radicals and dissenters who had fled the tyranny of the Old World, a refusal to grant visas to those whose ideas might be thought radical by the Daughters of the American Revolution; for faith in the wisdom of the people, a conviction that the people are children whose judgment is not to be trusted; for what Jefferson called "the illimitable freedom of the human mind," a deep distrust of freedom as something inescapably tarnished by subversion; for passion for peace and disarmament, an exaltation of the military and a readiness to rely on it without mercy or compassion.

Our search for peace is rooted in the assumption that we are—far more than other great nations—selfless, idealistic, and peace-loving. If this is indeed so, then it follows logically that the wars we fight must be an expression of those qualities. When we develop the most elaborate weapons system in the world, it is for peace; when we maintain 2,000 military establishments overseas, it is for peace; when we authorize the CIA to operate secretly in sixty countries and subvert those governments we do not approve of, it is for peace. We changed the government of Guatemala for peace, we invaded Cuba for peace, we landed marines in Santo Domingo for peace, we supported the Generals in Brazil and the Colonels in Greece and the colonialists in Portugal for peace; we came to the aid of Diem and Thieu for peace. Now that the war in Vietnam is over, we are bombing Cambodia every day as a kind of peace mission. What is most frightening about all this is that from

Mr. Nixon on down the American people can swallow this wonderland logic without gagging.

Nowhere is our changing sense of history more pronounced than in the changing attitudes of most Americans toward posterity. The generation whose bicentennial achievements we are about to celebrate was deeply and pervasively posterity-minded: the conviction that everything must be done for the benefit of future generations animated almost every one of the Founding Fathers. That attitude profoundly influenced the American concept of history too: though Old World nations were the prisoners of history, American was not; though in the Old World history is retrospective, in America it was prospective. Both these attitudes pretty well faded out in the past half century or so and now they are but a memory. Who now believes that America is the model for the world or that the new nations of India and Africa look to us for moral and spiritual guidance?

We early got into the habit of taking the future for granted. As President Wilson said in his first inaugural address, "We were very heedless, and in a hurry to be great." The passion to be great joined with the passion to be rich, to justify exploitation of those resources which should be the property of posterity, with almost unparalleled ruthlessness. What we sometimes overlook is that it is not only the material heritage we lay waste with our exploitations, our strip-mining, and our pollution, it is the political and the moral heritage as well. How little thought our government, our Corps of Engineers, our great corporations, our road builders and "developers" give to posterity; but how little thought, too, those who are prepared to sacrifice the Constitution, the Bill of Rights, the principle of due process of law, the ideal of even justice, the integrity of the ballot box, the dignity and privacy of the individual human being, give for posterity.

The growing habit of taking refuge in such terms as "national commitments," "national security," "obligations of power," "peace with honor," and in that jargon which burgeoned so luxuriantly during the Vietnam war—"free-fire zones," "protective aerial reaction," "surgical strikes," and "incontinent ordnance"—all this bespeaks a steady drift away from the world of realism to the world of self-delusion, from the inductive, the functional, the pragmatic in American thought to an indulgence in the abstract, the deductive and the doctrinaire.

The rationalization of the cold war, and of the Vietnam war, was rooted in this kind of abstraction. We conjured up a world conspiracy, a monolithic communism, a domino theory—what did we not conjure up?—without feeling any need to provide supporting evidence for our fears. President Nixon reduced the whole thing to a kind of obscene absurdity when he announced that the most powerful nation in the world would be a "helpless, crippled giant" if it could not invade Cambodia! It is the implications of that concept, the cost of that kind of thinking, that Senator Fulbright has explored with his customary lucidity, cogency and judiciousness, but with passion too. "This kind of thinking," he writes, "robs a nation's policy makers of objectivity and drives them to irresponsible behavior. The perpetuation of the Vietnam war is the most terrible and fateful manifestation of the determination to prove that we are 'Number One.'" And he reminds us that Assistant Secretary of Defense McNaughton's conclusion that "to avoid a humiliating United States defeat" accounted for some 70 percent of the logic of our war in Southeast Asia and inescapably should not suggest "a nation in thrall." We forget that thrall means slavery.

We have transferred this same psychology—and tactics —from the foreign to the domestic arena. In the realm of the law—the Dennis case is the most notorious example—we conjured up "conspiracy," searched out not dangerous acts but dangerous "tendencies," and created crimes almost as remote from reality as that of "imagining the death of the King." We took refuge in such public manifestations of patriotism as compulsory flag salutes, loyalty oaths, and the antics of the state and congressional un-American activities committees whose business was to provide "subversive" activities if they could not discover them, and who did.

Senator Goodell's account of the politicizing of our justice*—the resort to wiretapping, the use of provocative agents, the misuse of the grand jury, the readiness to prosecute as a kind of political punishment even when evidence of a crime was lacking—and sometimes to provide the evidence itself—all this is chilling and convincing. He was himself, he recalls, a victim of harassment: "When I was in the Senate, speaking out against administration policies, I learned that my official telephone was tapped and that Military Intelligence agents were following me around the country, building a dossier on my public remarks." He learned more about these techniques when he was counsel for Ellsberg in the Pentagon Papers case—the only criminal prosecution, he reminds us, in more than 4,000 instances of the violation of government regulations concerning classified materials. His book was written before the revelations of breaking into the office files of Ellsberg's psychiatrist, Dr. Fielding.

Even more sobering are two statements which the Senator quotes from men who occupied positions of great power. The first is from William Rehnquist, now sitting on the Supreme Court, who, when Assistant Attorney General, told the Senate Subcommittee on Constitutional Rights that the Constitution "empowers the President to prevent violation of law by maintaining surveillance of those who, *in his opinion, might* violate it" (italics mine). As no one over five

* *Political Prisoners in America* (New York, 1973).

can safely be excluded from this category we shall all have to engage in surveillance over each other. The second comes from the now happily retired Attorney General Kleindienst, who, in 1971, assured us that it would be unnecessary to suspend the Constitution in order to cope with political unrest because "there is enough play at the joints of our criminal law—enough flexibility—so that if we really felt that we had to pick up the leaders of a violent uprising we could. We would find some things to charge them with, and we would be able to hold them that way for a while."

Mr. Nixon and his attorneys general have indulged in the same kind of thinking, and used the same weapons; if the current *cri de coeur* is no longer simple communism or international conspiracy but "national security," the animus is the same, and the logic. The current phrase is potentially even more dangerous than its predecessors; it is broad enough to embrace supporting Pakistan against India, asking for prior censorship on the Pentagon Papers, resorting to wholesale wiretaps, authorizing mass arrests without warrants, burglaries corrupting the election process, secret agreements that imply, if they do not require, military commitments with Spain and Portugal—the list could go on and on. But as Governor Reagan has sagely observed, those guilty of misdeeds are not criminals, for they meant well. So, no doubt, did Benedict Arnold.

With growth, complexity and technological impersonality has come, almost inevitably, a weakening of individualism and of that "contrary-minded" quality which used to be so pronounced in the American character. This has meant a readiness to "follow the President on the ground that he must know best, to accept official handouts at face value, and to resent criticism of the government as something faintly unpatriotic. It has meant too a ready acquiescence in regimentation, manipulation and secrecy.

This attitude is not of course confined to military matters; it is even more flagrant in the readiness to accept the erosion of individual personality and the invasion of privacy in the world dominated by the computer. We are, statistically, far better educated than we were a century ago, but our education takes the form of thinking for ourselves rather less than it did a century ago. Whether because television has shortened our attention span, or the war benumbed our capacity for moral response, we were not seriously shocked by My Lai or wiretaps, or even by Watergate until it appeared to be connected with the White House. Many Americans see nothing wrong in political threats against newspapers and the television networks; indeed there is a kind of curious counter emotion that any paper criticism or even exposure is somehow unfair to the President.

We look with indifference too at the growth of what would once have been regarded as royal attributes in our rulers—the numerous luxurious residences they require, the special jet planes, the fleets of limousines, the vast entourage which accompanies them wherever they go. How odd to remember that when Thomas Jefferson walked back to his boardinghouse after giving his inaugural address, he could not find a seat available for him at the dinner table, or that a quarter century later President John Quincy Adams should have the same experience on a ship sailing from Baltimore to New York.

One of the most pronounced shifts in the American character appears to be the growth of a habit of mind that responds uncritically to manipulation. Advertising and "public relations" are the most familiar symbols—and instruments—of such manipulation. No previous administration has been so "public relations" minded or has relied so heavily on the manipulation of the public as Nixon's. Everything, so Mr. Nixon and his "team" seem to believe, can be manipulated: elections, justice, the economy, science, great issues of war and peace, the Constitution and the courts; it all depends on the "game plan," on your control of the media, and on your cunning.

Mr. Nixon thought that the Democratic party nomination could be manipulated—and perhaps he was right; that the election could be manipulated—and perhaps it was. Newspapers were not to be won over by sound policies and sound arguments but by petty pressures such as excluding reporters from social functions, and by powerful measures such as denying them access to information. Congress was to be won over not by arguments but by force or cunning, the courts by playing games with appointments—remember the Nixon caper of the six possible nominees to the Supreme Court. Justice is to be achieved by using provocative agents or rifling files; public-opinion polls are made by flooding the White House with phony telegrams; history by doctoring cables; the economy is directed by Alice in Wonderland statistics that never mean what they seem to mean. The President himself is to win the support of the people not through the force of his personality but by some "image" that is created for him.

Wars can be manipulated too, both for our side and for the enemy—thus the monthly assurance that the war in Southeast Asia was really over; thus the lies about the Vietnam invasion in 1964 and about Tonkin Gulf; thus the glowing picture of thousands of Asians from Korea to Australia fighting on our side, almost all of whom turned out to be mercenaries (we didn't use to like mercenaries, but that has changed); thus the notorious body counts which made clear that there were really no North Vietnamese males left to fight.

Supreme Court decisions, such as those on wiretapping and busing, can be manipulated to mean something different from what they seem to mean. The Constitution itself can be manipulated to prove the opposite of what the Founding

Fathers had written: thus the White House gloss on the war powers section, thus the invention of Executive "privileges" and "immunities." None of this would work if the American people had not been corrupted for more than a generation by the kind of advertising which floods all media day and night and whose essential principle is manipulation and seduction. A society trained to accept the preposterous claims, the deceptions, and the vulgarities of American advertising can perhaps be manipulated into accepting anything.

An administration which relies so largely on images and packaging and manipulation has neither respect nor capacity for larger ideas or views. In the end it may not be corruption but intellectual aridity that is the distinguishing feature of this administration.

These reflections raise more questions than they answer. We are confronted with the spectacle of corruption, a corruption not only moral and social but psychological and intellectual, confronted with a threat not only to the constitutional and political system but to constitutional and political thought. Where is the center of gravity? Is it in the White House? Is it in the Praetorian Guard that has infested the White House? Is it in the apparatus of secrecy we associate not only with the FBI and the CIA and with the Pentagon but with the whole of the administration? Or is there perhaps no center of gravity at all, no center of corruption even; do we have the sociological equivalent of Hannah Arendt's "banality of evil"?

Those guilty of what is moral treason to the Constitution, and of subverting the political system, are not evil conspirators, consciously bent upon destroying the America we have known. At the top they are the proud products of the American system of Private Enterprise, the very vindication of the American success story; those down the line are for the most part clean-limbed, clear-eyed, upstanding young men, the kind who figure in all our most stylish advertisements, the kind who are commonly voted "most likely to succeed" by their admiring classmates. These are not the makers and shakers of O'Shaughnessy's poem; they are the squares of the post-college generation. What kind of society is it that produces—and cherishes—men of these intellectual and moral standards? If our own conduct were scrupulous, if our own standards were honorable, would we really have permitted the Agnews and Mitchells and Magruders, the Deans and Haldemans and Kleindiensts to have imposed their moral standards upon us? Are we sure we have not imposed our moral standards upon them?

Our indignation and our outrage are both a bit shamefaced. After all, there is nothing new about the illegalities and immoralities of the Vietnam war; but we still tolerated the Cambodian war. After all, there is nothing new about the iniquities of the CIA; they have been going on now for almost twenty years, with scarcely a murmur of protest. After all, there is nothing new about the warnings of secrecy in government—that goes back 180 years to the principles of the Founding Fathers. After all, there is nothing new about the danger of the arrogance of power and the impropriety of using men and societies for our advantage; these go back to Kant's great categorical imperative. After all, there is nothing new about the moral that power corrupts—you can read that in Plutarch, if you ever bother to read Plutarch—or about warnings against imposing your will on weaker peoples—you can read that in Thucydides, if you bother to read Thucydides.

The Founding Fathers did read Plutarch and Thucydides. They knew that power tended to corrupt, and set up a system of checks and balances which they thought would protect the Commonwealth against that corruption. This administration has tried to paralyze those checks and balances—and who has protested? Who but a handful of journalists, senators and scholars?

The Founding Fathers knew instinctively what Montesquieu proclaimed in his *Spirit of the Laws,* that virtue is the animating principle of a republic. And to the Commonwealth they served—almost always at great personal sacrifice—they paid the tribute of virtue. But this administration which gibbers about "peace with honor" does not exalt virtue and does not practice it.

But do the people?

The Presidency
After Watergate

The Presidency has always given us trouble. It was, from the beginning, the "dark continent" of American constitutionalism—the phrase is Charles A. Beard's. There were ample precedents for the new legislative and judicial departments which the framers established, but none—except in a limited way in the states—for an elected executive who would serve at the pleasure of the people and on terms laid down by them. History, that great arsenal of morality, taught that all men in power were ambitious, vainglorious and corrupt and prone to arrogate power to themselves: you could read it in Thucydides or Plutarch, Montesquieu or Gibbon.

Contemporary experience reinforced the teachings of history, and the framers were determined that the United States should never have a Louis XIV to ruin his nation by his extravagance, a Frederick the Great to plunge his people into ceaseless wars, a George III to corrupt elections. As James Wilson, himself a strong-executive man, observed

First printed in slightly different form in *New York Review of Books,* October 18, 1973.

early in the Convention, he "did not consider the Prerogatives of the British Monarch as a proper guide in defining the Executive powers." All true enough. Yet after the near-breakdown of the Confederation, the nation needed a strong executive. And there was a further consideration—almost an embarrassment. Throughout the Convention, there sat George Washington presiding with awful dignity over the deliberations, the great man who would inevitably be the first President, whose rectitude was unassailable, and whose image would inevitably be reflected in the provisions for the presidential office.

As it turned out, lack of precedents and experience produced grave difficulties. Article II was the most debated and the least satisfactory part of the new Constitution. It emerged from the debates a kind of masterpiece of ambiguity and evasion whose meaning we have been exploring ever since. Not surprisingly, it has been modified by no fewer than four constitutional amendments—XII, XX, XXII and XXV—while only one amendment (XVII) has modified the legislative branch and one (XI, now universally forgotten) the judicial.

Because the powers of the President were not adequately defined, their character depended from the beginning on the Presidents who exercised them; that is why the game of classifying Presidents as "strong" or "weak," as "active-positive" or "passive-negative," has fascinated so many historians. Certainly Presidents can define the executive powers far more easily than the Congress or the courts can define theirs, for within the Presidency there is no competition, no rival party to bargain with or accommodate to. We do not define the legislative branch by Madison or Clay, Sumner or Blaine, nor do we define the judiciary by Marshall or Story, Holmes or Warren. But we do define the executive by analyzing Washington, Jackson, Lincoln, Wilson, Franklin Roosevelt and L. B. Johnson.

All strong Presidents have cultivated power, just as all strong judges have "soaked up jurisdiction like a sponge." Are we witnessing now a shift from cultivation to usurpation? The distinction, not always clear, is that the former functions within the hospitable and accommodating framework of the Constitution, and the latter does not. Washington, Lincoln and Franklin Roosevelt were indubitably "stronger" Presidents than Mr. Nixon, but Nixon is the first who has openly declared that he will not observe the constitional grant of war powers to the Congress and that he will not permit any interference with his own interpretation of "national security"; he is the first, too, to treat the guarantees of the Bill of Rights with open contempt.

In October of 1972, when the Senate was debating a proposal to permit the President to cut appropriations that Congress had voted, Senator Long of Louisiana said that "maybe the time has come when we need a benevolent dictator." This was not so much a speculation as a description, though not an accurate one, for even Mr. Nixon's uncritical admirers do not call him "benevolent." When we think of dictators, we conjure up Cromwell, Napoleon, Stalin or Hitler, and assure ourselves that it is improbable that one of these could ever emerge out of American politics. The traditional meaning of the term, however—that which traces back to ancien. nistory—is "one who is constitutionally or legally vested with supreme authority during a crisis." That is precisely what Senator Long had in mind and what Mr. Nixon is aiming at in some areas of government, certainly in the conduct of foreign affairs, of war and of whatever he chooses to believe involves national security—a supreme authority, which is above the law. It is this principle that enables him to countenance and his sycophantic subordinates to brush aside Watergate and the Ellsberg break-in, to authorize the use of *agents provocateurs*, flout congressional will in appropriations, wage secret war on a neutral country and then lie about it, conceal vital information from the people and from the Congress, and claim privileges and immunities heretofore unknown to the Constitution.

The Supreme Court disposed of these claims to be above the law first in the Milligan case of 1866 and then, some ninety years later, in the Youngstown steel case—a case which has interesting analogies to the invocation of independent war powers and national security arguments by Mr. Nixon today.

> The Constitution of the United States [said Justice Davis] is a law for rulers and for people, equally in war and in peace, and covers with the shield of its protection all classes of men, at all times and under all circumstances. No doctrine involving more pernicious consequences was ever invented by the wit of man than that any of its provisions can be suspended during any of the great exigencies of government. Such a doctrine leads directly to anarchy or despotism but the theory of necessity on which it is based is false; for the government, within the Constitution, has all the powers granted to it which are necessary to preserve its existence. (4 Wallace 2, 1866)

And in *Youngstown v. Sawyer,* which rejected President Truman's seizure of the steel mills on the ground of military necessity, Justice Black returned to the principle of Milligan:

> The contention is that presidential power should be implied from the aggregate of his powers under the Constitution. Particular reliance is placed on Article II which says that "the Executive Power shall be vested in a President," that he "shall take care that the laws be faithfully executed" and that he "shall be Commander-in-Chief of the Army and Navy of the United States." This order [Mr. Truman's take-over] cannot properly

be sustained because of the several constitutional provisions that grant executive power to the President. In the framework of our Constitution, the President's power to see that the laws are faithfully executed refutes the idea that he is to be a lawmaker. The Constitution limits his functions in the lawmaking process to the recommending of laws he thinks wise, and the vetoing of laws he thinks bad. And the Constitution is neither silent nor equivocal about who shall make laws which the President is to execute. (343 U. S. 579, 1952)

Now once again the great question of the scope, and the limit, of these powers is before the courts.

Over the years courts have been courageous and bold in the exercise of judicial review, as they were in the Milligan and the Youngstown steel cases, but is it a courage we can count on or a boldness we should ask them to display? Judges are understandably reluctant to intervene in the conduct of a war: as Justice Hughes once said, "The war power is the power to wage war successfully." The interventions usually, though not always, come well after the fact— as did that in the Milligan case. Traditionally, judges have avoided "questions of a political nature"—an avoidance less sweeping in the past two or three decades than in the more remote past. They are often troubled by the question of jurisdiction—as they are, even now, over the question of a subpoena of the executive tapes. And time and again they find themselves in the position of putting the stamp of constitutionality upon legislation or conduct which they disapprove on grounds of policy or of morals—as they did, for example, in the fugitive-slave cases and to some degree, in the Japanese-relocation cases.

Doubtless the deeply ingrained American instinct for putting controversial political and legal conduct to the constitutional test—which means the judicial test—is admirable; certainly it is instructive; it is also dangerous. It is admirable because it bespeaks a respect for the law and a conviction that the Constitution and the law are supreme and that no one, no matter how exalted, is above the law. It is instructive because it provides for the whole American people a continuous learned commentary on constitution and law, and on a great many other things as well; in the clarification of the never-ending problem of the relations of men to government, the United States Supreme Court is the greatest educational institution in history. It is dangerous because, over the years, it has substituted the criteria of legality for those of policy or wisdom; correctly so, for the function of the Court is legal, not moral.

As we tend to assume that an Act or an action which is unconstitutional is bad, and should therefore be rejected, so we conclude that one which somehow satisfies the criteria of constitutionality is good, and should be accepted. This is the position on which Mr. Nixon now takes his stand. He is not prepared to defend in principle such things as taping the conversations of his guests and associates, bombing Cambodia and then lying about it, or using provocative agents to instigate crime; instead he makes a great show of legal rectitude by shifting the whole question to constitutional grounds and claiming executive immunity to questions or to challenge.

In this sleight of hand he has been, so far, successful. He has the whole country talking about his constitutional right to protect the confidentiality of his tapes rather than asking why he made them in the first place; he has the country gravely considering whether his solemn obligation to protect the "national security" permits him to ignore ordinary constitutional limitations rather than asking what a civil war in Cambodia has to do with our national security or, for that matter, what the records of Mr. Ellsberg's psy-

chiatrist have to do with national security. If the historic
co roversy over Mr. Nixon's abuse of executive authority in
the foreign or the domestic arena bogs down in a debate
over constitutionality, it will achieve little except universal
exacerbation.

Ultimately there is no warranty for the principle of the
supremacy of the law, the integrity of the constitutional
fabric, and the successful functioning of the democratic
process except the virtue and intelligence of the American
people and of those they choose for high office. If these fail
us, nothing will succeed.

The question which confronts us now is whether the
constitutional crisis which Presidents Johnson and Nixon
have precipitated is a product of irresistible currents of history which cannot be deflected or reversed, or of the fortuitous conjunction of the cold war and the ten-year war in
Indochina and of two Presidents given to paranoia and ego-
mania. On the answer to this question will depend in large
measure our answer to the fateful query whether we can
return to our long tradition of constitutionalism or whether
we must resign ourselves to revolutionary changes in our
political system.

Hamilton, who wrote the *Federalist Papers* on Article II
of the Constitution, insisted that the most important quality
in a President was *energy*, and he defined energy as the
constitutional provision for unity, duration, adequate provisions for support, and competent powers. In this definition
Hamilton's customary habit of looking at all sides of a question failed him. The definition was circular, and the principle
misleading. Energy for what, and to what ends? After all,
there was no lack of energy in Frederick the Great or
Napoleon; in our own time there has been no lack of energy
in Hitler or Stalin. It is because Presidents Johnson and
Nixon have indulged their energies irresponsibly and pre-
sumptuously that the Presidency is in graver trouble today

than ever before in our history, and that the American Constitution is in trouble too.

The central principle of our constitutional system, as both Madison and James Wilson saw, is not energy but authority moderated by prudence, restrained by law, illuminated by reason, and animated by respect for freedom: in short, the reconciliation of freedom and order. It was to achieve this reconciliation that the Founding Fathers framed a constitution (the first of its kind in history) designed not only to form a more perfect union but to establish justice, promote the general welfare and secure the blessings of liberty. That was the end to which individual principles and mechanisms were made to contribute: separation of powers, checks and balances, distribution of governments among nation and states, bills of rights, judicial review. Thanks in large part to Presidents who used energy to ensure a more perfect union and to enlarge the area of freedom, this system of authority controlled by law survived the Civil War and the Great Depression and the Second World War without sacrificing the general welfare or betraying the liberties it was designed to safeguard. Can it survive the present crisis?

As soon as we ask this question we are conscious that it is rooted in disingenuousness and confesses a veneer of duplicity. For in fact the crises of the cold war and of the wars in Vietnam, Laos and Cambodia are not remotely like those of slavery and secession, or of the threat from the totalitarian world in 1940. By comparison with these, they are artificial and almost willful. We can see now—what sensible people saw twenty years ago—that China posed no threat to America or to legitimate American interests; certainly we can see now what the other signatories of SEATO saw from the beginning (all were equally bound by that treaty), that Vietnam and Laos posed no threat to the United States or to world peace.

So with most of the crises that have disfigured the history of the Nixon Administration. The crisis of "national security" posed by the publication of the Pentagon Papers was imaginary—no faintest hint of that threat to national security so hysterically invoked has yet emerged. The crisis of student protest and violence which Mr. Nixon recently invoked to justify such things as the Ellsberg break-in, and which Mr. Mitchell assumed extenuated the Kent State killings, was so artificial that when it died away of inanition the government had to reanimate it by the use of provocative agents. The fiscal crisis which led to the impounding of money voted by the Congress was phony; Mr. Nixon was prepared to spend twice as much new money on military weaponry and gadgetry as he proposed to save on medicine, welfare and education.

The crisis dramatized by Watergate—that of possible defeat at the polls—was one neither in principle nor in fact, but utterly contrived. It is absurd to say that the security of the nation was at stake in a Republican victory at the polls —and, after all, Nixon had the election in the bag. There was therefore no excuse even—we might say—on the criminal level for the extortion of millions of dollars in illegal or surreptitious campaign contributions, or for the whole bag of "dirty tricks" indulged in by Mr. Nixon's friends and associates. And the current crisis of the tapes too is something concocted out of fatuousness and guilt; it could have been avoided by refraining from making these indecent recordings in the first place.

Yet to meet these non-crises of his own making Mr. Nixon created a genuine crisis—one that goes far beyond the fate of his own Presidency and to the very nature of the institution itself. For to defend policies he never should have adopted, to justify misconduct he should have avoided, to claim powers he did not need and which he had no right to exercise, he contumaciously challenged principles of the supremacy of the law, the separation of powers, the probity of our system of justice and the integrity of the democratic process. This crisis is indeed ominous. Does it call for drastic remedies?

What remedies present themselves? We can persuade ourselves that the breakdown in the Presidency is a product of Mr. Nixon's malfeasance and impeach him and remove him from office. We can conclude that the presidential system, adequate for simpler days, is no longer competent to the problems that confront us, and turn to that parliamentary system which has proved widely successful and which the majority of the civilized nations of the globe now embrace. We can argue that the failure of the Congress to assert itself is not pathological but fortuitous, and that the mere reassertion of its power over the purse—where all that is needed is backbone—will restore that balance of power which was the original design of the framers. Or we can seek to write into the law or the Constitution additional safeguards against usurpation of power by Presidents.

It is by no means certain that impeachment would succeed, and certain that whether it does or not, it will further exacerbate rather than heal the deep rifts in our political and social fabric. It is wildly improbable that Americans would trade in a presidential system which has served them well for over a century and a half in exchange for a parliamentary one with which they have no experience, which is ill-adapted to the needs of federalism, and which has worked just as badly for many countries as its worst critics think the presidential system works in America.

A vigorous reassertion of the power of the purse would indeed go far to restore congressional authority and curb executive pretensions, but experience since Tonkin Bay (or perhaps since McKinley's Boxer expedition of 1900!) demonstrates that in times of foreign or military crisis the Congress is not disposed to call the President to account—or even to inquire too closely into the legitimacy of the crisis. Perhaps

the fourth remedy—additional safeguards against usurpation—holds out some promise of placing curbs on the executive which, by taking on the sober garb of the familiar and
the routine instead of the lurid robes of emergency, might
survive executive impetuousness, duplicity and corruption.
Catharsis and reform rather than convulsion and revolution
seem indicated.

A survey of the choreography between President and
Congress in the making of war (and of foreign policy) from
the beginning of our history to the present makes clear that
the early Presidents—those who had been schooled in the
great revolutionary debates and who had some experience
in state and national politics—scrupulously observed constitutional limitations on presidential war-making. The next
generation was not so fastidious, and the aggrandizement of
war-making powers can be dated from President Polk's
exploitation of the border dispute between Texas and Mexico
to foist a war on both countries. Lincoln's use of executive
power provides a unique chapter in presidential history—a
distinction, for example, between making or waging a foreign war and putting down a domestic insurrection, or that
between responding to an attack on United States soil and
carrying war to the territory of other countries. Thus it is
appropriate to draw moral lessons from the Lincoln experience with war, but not constitutional.

The modern history of executive usurpation begins with
the otherwise mild and innocuous McKinley, who fought
one unauthorized war in the Philippines and, without even
consulting the Congress, committed 5,000 troops to the
rescue of foreign legations in Peking at the time of the Boxer
uprising. President Wilson's record was surprisingly irregular
for so logical a man: he was high-handed in Mexico and the
Caribbean but legally scrupulous in his conduct toward the
European belligerents in the Great War. As for Franklin
Roosevelt, the crises which he faced were real—the crisis of

the depression and the greater crisis of the war. To meet the first he was—so he said—prepared to use extreme powers, but did not in fact do so. To meet the second, he did indeed strain the limits of Presidential authority—in the destroyer-bases deal, in the shoot-at-sight order, in the occupation of Iceland. It should be remembered, however, that he did not make his more extreme actions the bases for extreme claims of power, and that he always sought—and obtained—congressional approval for what he did.

How different the imperial claims of a Nixon. Much that he did, he did in secret: neither the public nor the Congress was permitted to know what he cared to do in the name of Presidential power or prerogative. What he did, he did indeed make the basis for further and bolder claims of power—in the realm of war, of almost limitless power. What he did, he did not choose to justify either to the Congress or the people—for instance, in the use of wiretaps or the subversion of the guarantees of the First Amendment. And what he did, he persisted in doing even after the Supreme Court had pronounced it improper. Other Presidents have stretched the bounds of the Constitution; Mr. Nixon alone has treated the Constitution with contempt.

Thus, for three-quarters of a century now there has been a fluctuating growth of presidential power. This process may continue, and while the Old World finds itself with monarchs who have neither the power nor the trappings of power, we may find ourselves with Presidents who have both to an extent beyond other heads of state in the Western world. Or are we perhaps on the verge of a shift in the nature and exercise of presidential power?

If that power depends so largely on war, will the end of our ten-year war in Asia and of the prospect of war among the great powers diminish the opportunity of exercising it? If much of the strength of Kennedy, Johnson and Nixon came, over the years, from their special role as cold warriors at a time when the country often seemed to be on the verge of nuclear war, will the thawing of the cold war and the growing improbability of nuclear war diminish the presidential role as champion of the "free world"? If domestic issues such as the control of environment, pollution, public health, zero population growth, poverty, urban renewal, and race problems, which demand professional expertise and bureaucratic efficiency, usurp the place of war and foreign affairs in the public mind, will not the center of political gravity shift from Presidents who bestride a world stage, no matter how awkwardly, to efficient managers who can solve unglamorous domestic problems?

If the impact—slower in coming than most of us thought —of *Baker v. Carr*, and the twenty-sixth amendment, the emergence of blacks as a genuine political force, the disillusionment of organized labor over the mismanagement of the economy all go to revive an opposition party and bring more independent politicians into the Congress, may we not see that branch reassert its legislative prerogatives, and thus weaken or diminish the role that the President may be expected to play? And finally, may not Watergate, with its sordid revelations of vulgarity, chicanery and blundering, spread such a sense of disillusionment through the body politic that voters will turn wearily from executive to legislative leadership—always assuming, to be sure, that the Congress can provide it? If so, we may be on the verge of a swing away from the full tide of executive power to ebb tide. If this is possible, it is too soon to write obituaries on the presidential system of government.

But to speculate on the future is hazardous; countervailing forces may prevail, and may serve to enhance rather than to contract executive power. There is, after all, no assurance that the détente between the United States and the Soviet Union will be permanent, nor is it clear that the United States has conclusively acknowledged the folly of her Asian policies over the past quarter-century and permanently abandoned the dream—or nightmare—of becoming an Asian power. Far more threatening in the long run is the upsurge of defiance and resolution among the impoverished nations of the globe, an upsurge whose strength and character was dramatically revealed in the recent meeting of seventy-six nations at the Algiers conference, whose theme was an end to the "pillage" of the globe by the great powers —particularly the United States.

The United States might be strong enough, independently, to resist, both materially and morally, pressure from fifty or sixty of the smaller unaligned nations, but can it resist pressure from the Arab nations which control most of the world's oil? Can it resist India, whose friendship it has all but forfeited by its demented policy of "tilting" toward Pakistan? Can it resist China if that behemoth throws its support to the underdeveloped nations and peoples of the world?

If the quarter century of cold war between the United States and the Communist nations is to be succeeded by a new cold war between the West and the rest of the world, all the considerations that produced the obsession with armaments and secrecy and the concentration of power in the executive will inevitably continue.

Nor is the threat wholly military. What if we continue to lay waste our natural resources of soil, water, timber, coal and oil, and come more and more to depend on outside contributions? What if our economy, staggering under the insensate demands of the military, and of the exploration of outer space, and the insatiable demands for an ever-higher standard of living and of growing inefficiency and wastefulness, cannot successfully compete with such nations as Japan and Germany, happily emancipated from the demands of the military, or with the European Common Market? Would not an economic crisis of this dimension enhance the executive power, much as the crisis of the Great Depression made possible—even inevitable—the enhancement of presidential power under Franklin Roosevelt?

Just as the best and perhaps the only way to curb presidential misuse of the war powers is to end the cold war and avoid violent war, so in the long run the only way to limit the abuse of presidential authority in domestic affairs may be to recognize the great revolution of three-fourths of the human race seeking, in one generation, to pull abreast of the rich and powerful nations of the West, and to join with them, and with the United Nations, to achieve a more just distribution of wealth and welfare, and an end to every kind of colonialism and imperialism.

It does not require much imagination to see the problems and perils that confront us, or much statesmanship to acknowledge the necessity of a multinational attack on those problems. Alas, the Nixon administration seems more prone to create and welcome crises that appear to require the enlargement of presidential powers than to work out solutions to those crises that might weaken the rationale for the exercise of these powers.

The Real Bases
for Impeachment

From the very beginning of the Watergate revelations, President Nixon has sought to paralyze or abort the operation of the constitutional provisions for impeachment by tactics of delay, evasion, confusion and deception, and by persuading the Congress and the American people that they should concentrate on narrow issues of legal crimes or on technicalities. Now there is serious danger that the House Impeachment Committee is prepared to endorse not Nixon's philosophy, but his tactics. It has allowed itself to be distracted from the contemplation of those "high crimes" which threaten the integrity of our constitutional system to crimes that are technical, low and vulgar. This is playing into Mr. Nixon's hands: if it is allowed to continue, the President may score not only a strategic and political victory, but a legal one.

The constitutional bases for impeachment are, or should be, clear enough, and so, too, the nature of those "high crimes" for which Mr. Nixon so richly deserves impeach-

First printed in slightly different form in *Newsday*, May 12, 1974.

ment. These are crimes against the commonwealth—the betrayal of trust, failure to preserve, protect and defend the Constitution, failure to take care that the laws are faithfully executed.

That impeachment and trial by the Senate are not directed to crimes in the ordinary sense of the term is clear from three elementary considerations in the process itself: first, that a verdict of guilty brings no kind of punishment, merely removal from office and disqualification for further public office; second, from the fact that the Founding Fathers, who wrote a prohibition of double jeopardy into the Bill of Rights, nevertheless provided that a President who was impeached and convicted might nevertheless be tried for crimes after his removal; and third, that by providing for trial by the Senate, they distinguished impeachable crimes from all others where, in every case, "the accused shall enjoy the right of a speedy and public trial by an impartial jury. . . ."

On the positive side, all the evidence we have from the authors of the Constitution makes clear that what they had in mind when they drafted and voted on the provisions for impeachment in the Constitution was what had been long familiar in English law and history, and what was even then being illustrated in the great trial of Warren Hastings over in London. It was put well by the great Edmund Burke. He said:

> It is by this process that statesmen who abuse their power, are accused by statesmen and tried by statesmen, not upon the niceties of a narrow jurisprudence but upon the enlarged and solid principles of state morality. It is here [in the Commons] that those who by the abuse of power have violated the spirit of the law, can never hope for protection from any of its forms. It is here that those who have refused to conform them-

selves to its perfections, can never hope to escape
through any of its defects.

What the framers had in mind, in short, was precisely those
"political crimes" which Mr. Nixon is so anxious to rule out
of consideration and which Mr. St. Clair, in an argument
which would disgrace any schoolboy, has declared to be
outside the scope of impeachment.

So said the three men who contributed most to the
making and the explanation and elucidation of the Constitution: James Madison, the "Father of the Constitution";
Alexander Hamilton, who wrote the essays on the Presidency in the *Federalist Papers;* and James Wilson, who
steered ratification of the Constitution through the Pennsylvania ratifying convention, served on the first Supreme
Court of the United States and delivered the first formal
lectures on the Constitution at the University of Pennsylvania.

Listen to Madison: In the Federal Convention, he said (it
was on 20 July, 1787) that it was "indispensable that some provision should be made for defending the Community against
the *incapacity, negligence or perfidy* of the Chief Magistrate." In the first Congress, arguing the necessity to give
the President power to remove his subordinates, he observed
that this "would make him in a peculiar manner, responsible
for their conduct, and subject him to impeachment himself
if he suffers them to perpetrate with impunity high crimes
or misdemeanours against the United States or neglects to
superintend their conduct or to check their excesses. . . ."
And in the debate on the creation of a department of foreign
affairs, he added that "if the President acted so as to displace
from office a man whose merits require that he should
continue in it [Mr. Cox, perhaps?] he will be impeachable
by the House before the Senate against such an act of mal-
administration, for I contend that the wanton removal of

meritorious officers would subject him to impeachment and removal."

Listen to Hamilton, in number 65 of the *Federalist Papers*, discussing the duties of the Congress when constituted a court for impeachment: "The subjects of its jurisdiction are those offenses which proceed from the misconduct of public men, or in other words from the abuse or violation of some public trust. They are of a nature which may, with peculiar propriety, be denominated *political*, as they relate chiefly to injuries done immediately to society itself. . . ."

Or listen to James Wilson, discoursing on the Constitution at the University of Pennsylvania: "In the United States . . . impeachments are confined to political characters, to political crimes and misdemeanors, and to political punishments."

Nor did subsequent commentators differ from these great authorities. Of all the commentators on the Constitution, it was Joseph Story, who had sat with John Marshall upon the Supreme Court, and whose Commentaries on the Constitution have been cited by the Supreme Court as authoritative in many areas for almost a century and a half, whose judgment was most respected. Here he is discussing the grounds for impeachment in English law, and in American. It will be found, he says, "that many offenses, not easily definable by law, and many of a purely political character, have been deemed high crimes and misdemeanors worthy of this extraordinary remedy. Thus . . . where a Lord Chancellor has been thought to have put the great seal to an ignominious treaty; a Lord Admiral to have neglected the safeguard of the sea; an Ambassador to have betrayed a trust; a privy counsellor to have propounded or supported pernicious doctrines and dishonorable measures; or a confidential advisor of his sovereign to have obtained exorbitant grants . . . these have all been deemed impeachable offenses." Such impeachments, Story added, might well be considered harsh, but perhaps necessary. "But others again were founded on the most salutary public justice, such as impeachment for malversions and neglects of office; . . . for official oppression, extortions and deceits; and especially for putting good magistrates out of office and advancing bad. . . . One cannot," he added, "but be struck with the utter unfitness of the common tribunals of justice to take cognizance of such offenses; and with the entire propriety of confiding the jurisdiction over them to a tribunal capable of understanding and reforming and scrutinizing the polity of the state; and of sufficient dignity to maintain the independence and reputation of worthy public officers."

Even more relevant to the current situation is Story's conclusion that "an impeachment is a proceeding purely of a political nature. It is not so much designed to punish an offender, as to secure the state against gross official misdemeanors. It touches neither his person nor his property, but simply divests him of his official capacity."

Let us return then to what Edmund Burke called the Grand Inquest of the nation: an exercise of sovereignty at once dignified, elevated and solemn, and one which takes on deep significance when we contemplate how most peoples and nations, throughout the whole of history, have rid themselves of rulers in whom they had lost confidence. The process of constitutional impeachment is, we should remember, one of the many ways in which Americans have legalized and institutionalized revolution. It is an essential part of the very American system of checks and balances; it is an essential device for limiting and rebuking the pretensions of power and the abuse of power; it is an essential ingredient in constitutionalism.

It would be a pity to impeach Mr. Nixon on grounds that are technical, trivial or vulgar: if such offenses are all that is involved, the nation could afford to wait three more years for the moment when Mr. Nixon would be automatically retired to that private life which he so richly merits. Trivial or technical crimes do not threaten the integrity of the Constitution, the sanctity of the Bill of Rights, the safety of the Republic. But "high crimes" do threaten all three.

It is important then, that Mr. Nixon be impeached and tried for high crimes. What are the high crimes which may justly be charged against him, and on which he should be tried?

First, the illegal and secret war against Cambodia. The Constitution is clear on the war powers: it is the Congress that is authorized to declare war, not the President, and no arguments of "national security" can change that elementary fact. Its illegality in the eyes of international law is as clear as its illegality in American law: if China—which was supporting the North Vietnamese as we the South, had chosen to fly 3,500 bombing missions over Southern California on the ground that the area was supplying the South Vietnamese with weapons (which it assuredly was), we would not be very patient with the argument that this was merely a diversionary gesture to slow up supplies, and should not be considered an act of war.

Second, to compound the crime of the Cambodian War, Mr. Nixon lied not only to the American people but to the Congress. But the Constitution confers the war power on the Congress, as it confers on Congress the power to appropriate money for war. To deceive the American people about a matter of such prodigious importance is clearly immoral. To deceive a coordinate branch of the government—one with a constitutional obligation to participate in the conduct of foreign affairs and of war—is just as clearly unconstitutional.

Third, Mr. Nixon has chosen to "impound" some fifteen billions of dollars constitutionally appropriated by the Congress for specific programs. Centuries of history look down upon us when we contemplate this particular "high crime" —a history of the long and arduous struggle of the Commons against Tudor and Stuart monarchs for the control of the purse, and of the struggle, too, of American colonial legislatures against Royal governors for the same objective. The Founding Fathers were determined that the hardly won power over the purse should never be frittered away, and they wrote it into the Constitution. Now confronted by Congressional votes overriding his vetoes of appropriation bills, Mr. Nixon has resorted to what he calls "impoundment": that is, he refuses to spend money which Congress has appropriated as the Congress wants it spent. What he presents to us here is a twofold violation of the Constitution: first, a nullification of the constitutional provisions giving to the Congress power to appropriate money, and second, a nullification of the constitutional provisions governing the exercise of the presidential veto and providing the method whereby the Congress can override the veto. If Mr. Nixon can substitute "impoundment" for a veto in the matter of appropriations he can, presumably, do so in any other matter, and he has therefore amended the Constitution itself.

Fourth, Mr. Nixon has repeatedly and contumaciously flouted, ignored, circumvented and nullified the guarantees of the Bill of Rights. A large subject this, and it must suffice to list some of the more spectacular examples of Mr. Nixon's impeachable offenses here:

1. The attempt to apply—for the first time in all of our history—prior censorship to newspapers in order to prevent them from printing the Pentagon papers.

2. The mass roundup and arrest of some twelve thousand Americans exercising their constitutional right of peaceable assembly and petition in their capital city on May Day of 1971. The arrests were made without warrants; those arrested were denied the right to consult lawyers or to know the charges against them, and were illegally detained. Within a day, to be sure, all but some thirty or forty were released

—again without charges against them. There was no declaration of a national emergency; there was no suspension of the writ of habeas corpus; there was, in short, no legal justification for the arrests. This was the naked face of the police state.

3. The widespread and continuous use of that most hated device of the police state—the provocative agent, whose business it is to instigate others to commit crimes and then expose them. This was what we know happened to the Gainesville Eight, to the Camden Nine, to Father Philip Berrigan and to many others; how widespread the use of the provocative agent we do not yet know, but we may well believe that what we have seen is only the top of the iceberg.

4. The use of electronic surveillance—wiretaps—in literally scores of instances, contrary to the constitutional prohibition of unreasonable search and seizure as interpreted by the Supreme Court. It is Mr. Nixon's unenviable distinction that his administration may be remembered chiefly as the "wiretap" presidency; everyone in it—and outside it—was apparently "bugged," including even members of the National Security Council. Wiretapping itself is only one manifestation of wholesale invasions of the privacy of the citizen: add to it—with Presidential approval—eavesdropping, military spying, burglary, intimidation of the press and other media—all designed to curb the exercise of those great freedoms guaranteed in the Constitution—freedom of speech, of the press and of petition, and to impair that right which now has constitutional recognition—the right of privacy. Nor is the nature of these violations of the laws left to conjecture: the Federal Criminal Code (Section 241) provides that any one who "conspires to injure, oppress, or intimidate any citizen in the free exercise or enjoyment of any right or privilege secured to him by the Constitution or laws of the United States, or because of his having exercised the same" is guilty of a crime.

5. Finally, by resort to "dirty tricks"—fabricating scandalous stories about political opponents, systematic espionage on political rivals, compiling "enemies lists," punishing civil servants who asked embarrassing questions about official malpractices, raising money corruptly from corporations and spending it corruptly to influence elections—Mr. Nixon has attempted the corruption not only of the constitutional system but of those political processes which have come to be an integral part of that constitutional system and essential to its effective working. To instill in the American people a contempt for parties and politics is to encourage contempt for democracy itself, and that is certainly a dereliction of duty and a betrayal of faith.

What this record discloses is precisely those high crimes and misdemeanors which, as far as we know, the Founding Fathers had in mind when they put the impeachment clause into the Constitution: the violation of the principle of the separation of powers, the undermining of the legislative and even the judicial power in many areas, the usurpation of the great power to make war and the historic power of congressional control of the purse; the claim of "inherent" power to do anything and everything necessary to what he deems "the national security"; the subversion of many of the guarantees of the Bill of Rights; the use of money, trickery and chicanery to corrupt elections, and the deliberate degradation of the political processes essential to the effective working of our democracy. It is for these crimes that the House should impeach and the Senate try Richard Nixon.

Two Postscripts

The Constitution Vindicated

We have had constitutional crises before, but except
for the Civil War and Reconstruction, none that had the
dimensions of those precipitated by Richard M. Nixon. Never
before have we had a crisis that challenged the basic assumptions of our constitutional system itself, and the basic processes and mechanisms through which it worked.

Alexander Hamilton, though he supported the Constitution, thought it "a frail and worthless fabric" and had no
confidence that it would endure. And no wonder. It was,
after all, without precedent or model in history. Never before
had a people made a national constitution; never before had
they fabricated a federal system; never before had they
elected a national head of state; never before had they fixed
effective limits on government by such devices as a genuine
separation of powers and bills of substantive rights that had
the force of law.

Almost miraculously, the system worked. The "frail
and worthless fabric" proved to be both tough and enduring

From *The New York Times*, August 11, 1974.

153

and, what is more astonishing, proved wonderfully resilient. Under its auspices the United States grew from thirteen to fifty states; under its auspices it weathered one crisis after another, and that without suspending any of its great provisions, without impairing the authority and dignity of the Presidency, the power of the Congress or the independence of the judiciary.

In 1861 the South challenged the Constitution and set up on its own; then it honored the document by transforming it, with only minor changes, into a constitution for the Confederacy.

The Constitution survived the First World War; the crisis of the Great Depression and the challenge of the welfare state; the unprecedented strains of the Second World War.

One reason the Constitution survived intact was that no President had ever attempted to subvert it; no politicians—with the exception of Aaron Burr—had even threatened it.

Notwithstanding the absence of any tradition of loyalty to the new government, the United States, even in infancy, did not have a Cromwell, nor, in maturity, a Hitler.

Here—for perhaps the first time in modern history—it was not necessary to call upon loyalty to a king to preserve the commonwealth.

As Tom Paine put it, "Where then is the King of America? Know that in America the Constitution is King."

Or as Thomas Jefferson wrote, after he and Hamilton had frustrated Burr's attempt to steal the election of 1800:

> The tough sides of our Argosy had been thoroughly tried. Her strength has stood the waves into which she was steered, with a view to sink her. We shall put her on her republican tack and she will show by the beauty of her motion, the skill of her builders.

For the first time since 1861, an administration, Mr. Nixon's, called into question both the beauty of her motion and the skill of her builders. For what is it that has been at stake for the last two years—what but the integrity and the vitality of the Constitution itself and of the principles it is designed to secure: a more perfect union, justice, domestic tranquillity, the blessings of liberty and the rule of law?

Let us be more specific.

First. The principle of a government of laws and not of men—a principle so precious that the Founding Fathers wrote it into many of the state constitutions. By countenancing burglary, wiretapping, *agents provocateurs*, the use of the Federal Bureau of Investigation, the Central Intelligence Agency and even the Internal Revenue Service to punish "enemies," by endorsing the Huston Plan for the creation of a police state and by resort to secrecy, duplicity and deception in the operations of government, Mr. Nixon sought to substitute his own fiat for the law.

Second. The principle, vindicated by the United States Supreme Court in the great case of *ex parte* Milligan:

> The Constitution is a law for rulers and people, equally in war and in peace, and covers with the shield of its protection all classes of men at all times and under all circumstances. No doctrine involving more pernicious consequences was ever invented by the wit of man than that any of its great provisions can be suspended during any of the great exigencies of government.

By creating sham "exigencies" involving "national security," Mr. Nixon sought to justify the violation of constitutional guarantees of due process, of the fundamental rights of citizens and of the welfare of society, and authorized withholding of evidence essential to justice—in effect suspending vital provisions of the Constitution.

Third. The principle of the separation of powers, a principle established first by Americans as the most effective method of holding each branch of government within the framework of the Constitution.

By usurping congressional power to declare war, making war on neutral Cambodia and concealing that war from the Congress and the American people; by shrouding much of the conduct of foreign affairs in a fog of secrecy, denying to the Congress information essential to the faithful performance of its constitutional duties, and by nullifying Congressional power over appropriations through the device of impounding funds duly voted by the Congress, Mr. Nixon undermined the integrity of this great principle.

Fourth. The principles of freedom and justice in the Bill of Rights. By attempting to impose, for the first time in our history, prior censorship of the press, by threatening hostile television stations with deprivation of their licenses, by directing the arrest without warrants of some 12,000 men and women gathered in the capital city to exercise their constitutional rights of assembly and petition, by flouting the constitutional prohibition against unreasonable search and seizure and the requirement of search warrants and by ignoring the provisions for due process of law in the endorsement of the Huston Plan and in the illegal use of the Central Intelligence Agency in domestic affairs, Mr. Nixon presented the most dangerous threat to the Bill of Rights in the whole of our history.

Fifth. The integrity and survival of democratic government in the United States.

By corrupting presidential elections through the solicitation of illegal contributions, by a systematic campaign of mendacity, trickery and character assassination against opponents and by violating the integrity of the civil service and corrupting his closest subordinates, Mr. Nixon gravely endangered the integrity of our republican system of government.

Mr. Nixon's resignation is no voluntary act. It was not inspired by contrition or by a belated loyalty to the Constitution. It was forced on him by a ground swell of public outrage, by a popular rallying to the Constitution comparable to that which swept the North at the time of Fort Sumter and by a Congress that after long vacillation finally responded to the standards of duty and the obligations of the Constitution.

The long-drawn-out process of inquiry by committee, by the courts and by the Congress is a stunning vindication of our constitutional system, a vindication of the principle of separation of powers, of the independence of the courts and of the foresight of the framers.

The men who made our Constitution were familiar with the history of executive tyranny. They were steeped in the history of the ancient world and knew well the story of usurpation of power, revolution and assassination in the city-states of Greece and in Rome.

They knew, too, the tragic history of England and the fate of a Richard II, a Mary Queen of Scots and a Charles I; they had themselves just fought a war against what they thought to be the tyranny of George III. They were determined to write a new page in history, and did. They accepted the necessity of change in government and in leadership. They invented the great institution of the constitutional convention—a legal way to alter and abolish government and institute new government.

They took over the English practice of impeachment and applied it to their highest office, providing a legal and peaceful method of removing the President himself from office.

Thus, in the words of Alexander Hamilton, they "substituted the mild magistracy of the law for the terrible weapon of the sword."

Confronted, for the first time in our long history, with a chief magistrate who betrayed his oath of office, we have resorted to that "magistracy of the law" and vindicated once again the wisdom of the Founding Fathers. Thus, we have demonstrated to the world and, let us hope, to future generations that the Constitution is alive and well, that it can be adapted to the exigencies of governance and that in an emergency an enlightened and determined democracy can protect and defend its principles, its honor and its heritage.

When, on September 17, 1787, members of the Federal Convention came forward to sign the Constitution that they had drafted during those long hot months in Philadelphia, the venerable Dr. Franklin arose and,

> looking toward the president's chair, at the back of which a rising sun happened to be painted, observed that painters had found it difficult to distinguish in their art between a rising and a setting sun. "I have often and often," said he, "in the course of the session and the vicissitudes of my hopes and fears as to its issue looked at that sun behind the presidency, without being able to tell whether it was rising or setting. Now at length I have the happiness to know that it is a rising and not a setting sun."

Learning from the Tragedy

Watergate was a tragedy, but not an unmitigated one. Already it is clear that we have learned much from it; we can almost say that we have profited from it. Right now we look back at it with astonishment: How did we ever allow it to happen? In a few years we will look back on it with a certain pride because we did not in fact succumb to what happened, or allow ourselves to be overwhelmed or subverted by it. On the contrary, before the situation got hopelessly out of hand, we rallied our resources, rejected it and reversed it.

Watergate—I use the term as a symbol—was an attempt to subvert the Constitution, but the Constitution survived. It was an attempt by the President to put himself above the law, but in the end it was the law that imposed its magisterial authority upon the President. It was an attempt to nullify important guarantees in the Bill of Rights, but the guarantees survived and helped to keep alive those freedoms which in the end brought down the President. It was an attempt to

This chapter appeared, in slightly revised form, in *Time*, August 19, 1974.

159

break down the separation of powers, reduce the Congress to impotence and paralyze the machinery of justice, but the Congress discovered its sense of responsibility, and the courts maintained their independence. It was an attempt to cripple the political processes of our democracy and of our party system, but these recovered and proved themselves resilient and tenacious. It was an attempt to deceive the people through secrecy and fraud, but in the end Lincoln's aphorism about fooling all the people all the time was vindicated.

Thus, once again, as three times in our past when we faced great crises—the attempt by Aaron Burr to steal the election of 1800, the Civil War and the Great Depression— the Constitution and the political processes that it nourished proved themselves tough and enduring. Without disorder, confusion or even excessive bitterness, we have quietly forced Mr. Nixon out of office and quietly installed Mr. Ford. This is a revolution. In most countries of the globe it would be a violent revolution, but in the United States it is peaceful and legal. It is indeed constitutional revolution, for just as the Founding Fathers invented the constitutional convention as a legal method of altering or abolishing government and instituting a new one, they and their successors also devised the complex process of impeachment, resignation and succession as a constitutional method of removing a head of state and installing his successor.

Thus at every stage of Watergate and the "Grand Inquest" that followed, we have a vindication of the Constitution and of the political habits that have grown up under it. And this has brought with it a large measure of popular education in constitutionalism, in the meaning of separation of powers, in the central importance of the Bill of Rights and in the validity and resourcefulness of the democratic process. The purpose of impeachment is not only to remove from office a man who has betrayed the public trust. It is also to explore the nature of that public trust, and to make clear what it means to preserve, protect and defend the Constitution of the United States.

Some questions that should have been settled remain, to be sure, unsettled: the question of presidential war-making, for example, or of the reach of presidential privileges and immunities, or of the balance (if any) between the claims of national security and the guarantees of the Bill of Rights. It is by no means clear, however, that impeachment would have settled these questions; but it is highly probable that for all practical purposes they have been answered by public opinion. It is wildly improbable that President Ford or his successors in the foreseeable future will wage war on a neutral country, impound congressional appropriations, interfere with the processes of justice, openly flout the guarantees of freedom of speech and of the press or seek to establish a police state—all of which Mr. Nixon did. Impeachment by an informed public opinion has provided guidelines for the future as effective as those which might have emerged from the trauma of an impeachment trial.

The expulsion of Richard Nixon and the repudiation of his impudent claims to privilege, prerogatives and power will have a restorative effect on the whole body politic. It will go far to reestablish that equality and balance of the three departments of government so central to the thinking of the Founding Fathers. The process has indeed already begun: the Congress declared its independence in its conduct of the abortive impeachment proceedings; the Court affirmed its independence with a unanimous vote on the validity of presidential subpoenas. We should add that the fourth estate—the press—proudly maintained its independence in the face of almost intolerable pressures, seductions and intimidations.

The removal of Mr. Nixon will go far to restore the integrity of the American political system. Though his whole adult life had been devoted to politics, he seemed to have no appreciation of the delicate and peculiar nature of the system or of the historic role of political parties in maintaining and working it. Instead, he was prepared to corrupt parties, corrupt the CIA, the FBI and the IRS, corrupt his own associates, corrupt the press, deceive the public and buy elections. But it was, in the long run, public outrage at the prostitution of politics for private and partisan purposes that destroyed Mr. Nixon's credibility and forced his resignation. If, in the future, ambitious politicians take this lesson to heart, democracy will function better because of Watergate.

Now that Watergate and Mr. Nixon are behind us, President Ford has set himself to bind up the wounds that they inflicted. With malice toward none, with charity for all, we must cooperate in this honorable task. Then we can return to a consideration of those great issues of domestic and world politics that we have sorely neglected, or allowed to go by default. Not only have the issues been neglected, but Watergate and all that it involved has tended greatly to magnify the importance of domestic as contrasted with global problems. It has, too, magnified purely political issues. These are issues that were in their very nature fortuitous, issues that should never have come up and were in themselves unworthy of the attention of a mature people: corruption, chicanery, mendacity, duplicity, ward politics and private spite.

Now, under new leadership, we may be able to turn our attention to those global problems which glare at us from every quarter of the horizon, and which must be solved if we, and the rest of mankind, are to survive: the exhaustion of natural resources, energy and food; the pollution of water and of air; the imminent doubling of the world's population in the next half century, with its threat of mass starvation and of wars for survival; the control of the weather, which is a potential weapon of national aggrandizement and of warfare; the necessity for an abatement of traditional nationalism and for some form of international control over the distribution of food and other resources; the elimination of the threat of biological warfare; the regulation of the use and misuse of atomic power and the end of the exploitation of weak and little nations by the strong.

This is a heady agenda. It is by no means clear that Mr. Ford or the Congress will embrace it: Mr. Ford is, after all, traditionally a militarist and a hawk, and the Congress has been, for the past decade, almost as chauvinistic as the President. But at least we now have a better chance to consider these global problems in an atmosphere of nonpartisanship than we did while engaged in the elementary though essential task of salvaging our political and constitutional system. For too long now our center of gravity has been Washington. Now we must all realize that our center of gravity is the globe.

A Note About the Author

HENRY STEELE COMMAGER did his graduate work in history at the Universities of Chicago and Copenhagen. From 1926 to 1938 he taught American history at New York University and for the next two decades was Professor of History at Columbia University. In 1956 he became Smith Professor of History at Amherst College, where he now holds the position of Simpson Lecturer. Mr. Commager has held the Pitt Chair of American History at Cambridge University, the Harmsworth Chair at Oxford University and the Gottesman Chair at Uppsala University, and has taught at numerous universities in the United States and Europe over the past forty years. He is an Honorary Fellow of Peterhouse, Cambridge, and holds an Honorary Professorship at the University of Santiago de Chile. In 1972 he was awarded the Gold Medal for History by the American Academy of Arts and Letters. Among his numerous books are *Theodore Parker: Yankee Crusader*, *The American Mind*, *Majority Rule and Minority Rights*, *The Search for a Usable Past*, *Britain Through American Eyes*, *The Blue and the Gray*, *Documents of American History*, *The Commonwealth of Learning*, *Jefferson, Nationalism and the Enlightenment*, and with Samuel Eliot Morison, *The Growth of the American Republic*, generally recognized as a classic in its field.